THE PRENTICE-HALL SERIES IN FAMILY AND CONSUMER SCIENCES

WILLIAM H. MARSHALL, *editor*
The University of Wisconsin, Madison

nutrition, behavior, and change
HELEN H. GIFFT
MARJORIE B. WASHBON
GAIL G. HARRISON

introduction to family life and sex education
ROSE M. SOMERVILLE

the visible self: perspectives on dress
MARY ELLEN ROACH
JOANNE B. EICHER

THE VISIBLE SELF

THE VISIBLE SELF:
Perspectives on Dress

MARY ELLEN ROACH
University of Wisconsin, Madison

JOANNE B. EICHER
Michigan State University, East Lansing

PRENTICE-HALL, INC., ENGLEWOOD CLIFFS, NEW JERSEY

Library of Congress Cataloging in Publication Data

ROACH, MARY ELLEN.
  The visible self.

  (The Prentice-Hall series in family and consumer sciences)
  Includes bibliographical references.
  1. Costume. 2. Clothing and dress—Psychology.
I. Eicher, Joanne B., joint author. II. Title.
GT521.R57   391   72-11966
ISBN 0-13-942284-6

© 1973 by Prentice-Hall, Inc., Englewood Cliffs, New Jersey

Printed in the United States of America

10 9 8 7 6 5 4 3 2 1

prentice-hall international, inc., london
prentice-hall of australia, pty. ltd., sydney
prentice-hall of canada, ltd., toronto
prentice-hall of india private limited, new delhi
prentice-hall of japan, inc., tokyo

CONTENTS

ILLUSTRATIONS

Chapter 5

Chapter 6

Chapter 7

25) is a feminine trait, with a rare exception being the male Mohave Indians. The deep squat (26, 27, and 28) is uncomfortable for adult Europeans, but replaces the sitting posture for at least a fourth of mankind. The last two rows show various asymmetrical postures.

Chapter 8

Chapter 9

Chapter 10

Chapter 13

acknowledgments

Many people—family members, colleagues students, friends, secretaries, and sometimes strangers and chance acquaintances—have contributed both consciously and unconsciously to the content of this book. They have helped us in the generation and development of ideas, as well as in the everyday mechanical details of manuscript preparation, by providing everything from a stimulating critique of the manuscript to a reference or suggestion for an illustration. All of these people we thank; a few we take the opportunity to give special acknowledgments. Ann Slocum's chapter on *The Economic Dimensions of Dress* provided us with a much desired broad perspective on the capabilities of countries with various kinds of resources and various kinds of economies to deliver clothing for human use. Holly Schrank has not only been an invaluable colleague in testing ideas, but has also enhanced the usefulness of the book by writing the teacher's manual. This manual incorporates many creative yet practical ideas for utilization of the book as a textbook in classes that introduce the subject of dress as an academic discipline or are devoted to the topic of world dress.

Much appreciated are the useful criticisms of early drafts of various chapters made by Ann Creekmore, Marilyn DeLong, Kathleen Ehle, Thomas J. Higgins, Ruth Nielsen, Margaret Warning, Betty Wass, and Tom Witt.

Many thanks to Carl Eicher whose willingness to carry out a wide variety of supportive activities, both professional and domestic, helped us to initiate and complete the manuscript.

Very special thanks must go to Jean Grof for her many skills and for being available at the crucial times when editing, library searching, manuscript typing, letter writing, proofreading, and other kinds of work concerned with manuscript preparation were needed.

PREFACE

The relationships between human beings and their dress are the focus of this book. Each person is a biological, aesthetically sensitive, and social being; the visible self—body and dress—reflects this fact. Today, as through the ages, dress is an individual's most immediate environment, acting as buffer between the biological self and the wider physical environment; in addition, dress often delights the individual because it beautifies and provides a link with other individuals in many festive, ceremonial, and everyday activities. As it performs these services, dress covers and decorates the body. Covering and decorating can only arbitrarily be separated from each other: that which covers provides some decoration and that which decorates usually provides some minimum cover. In addition, although body ornament and cover may differ greatly in form, they may function for human beings in very similar ways.

Thus, even when a coronation robe primarily covers and a jewelled crown ornaments, each shows to observers the high status of the wearer and presumably provides the individual with feelings of personal worth. Similarly, a decorative amulet worn to ward off evil spirits may be considered just as important for protection as an all-enveloping space suit.

The simplest, least arbitrary definition of dress, therefore, groups together all kinds of body ornamenting and covering as part of dress, and makes clear that the process of dressing one's self includes diverse activities: arranging of hair; donning of jewelry and other accessories; investing with robes, tunics, aprons, and trousers; painting, scarring, tattooing the skin; chipping or staining of teeth; stretching of earlobes or lips; binding of waists or feet. So defined, dress need not be distinguished from *costume* or even *clothing*, often defined narrowly as covering only. All three terms can be defined broadly to include both body covering and ornament and therefore are interchangeable; however, we prefer the term dress as the most comprehensive word. Special concern with either covering or ornament is made clear by context or unique emphasis.

We have made special effort to consider dress of different age, sex, national, racial, and ethnic groups. We have also endeavored to encourage a broad view by citing a variety of non-American and non-Western examples of dress, as well as American and Western.

The main purpose of this book is to introduce a new perspective for understanding why people dress as they do. The first section summarizes the development through the years of ways of describing form of dress and ways of interpreting various social, cultural, and psychological aspects of dress. The perspective presented is unique, since up until this time no synthesis of this information has been attempted. In Section II biological similarities and differences in appearance are considered as well as the relation of dress to body functioning, comfort, and health. Dress is considered both as environment and as means of intervening between the body and environment.

Section III emphasizes that aesthetic expression through the use of dress plays a part in lives of people everywhere, that an understanding of the aesthetic act of dressing requires knowledge of the connection between cultural setting and individual display, and that promotion of any particular standard for dress has meaning only within the society in which it emerges. To some extent decisions on how to react to standards for dress—to utilize, accommodate to, ignore, reject, or oppose, for example—are always the choice of the individual, as he perceives his own needs within his particular social context. However, his society may greatly limit the range of his action. One society may be very permissive and encourage much variety and individual uniqueness; another may limit actions and prescribe very specifically what dress will be for different individuals and social categories.

The dress of each person depends on a number of environmental circumstances; however, certain factors are critical in contemporary world society. In the first place, systems of rational thought based on scientific inquiry, and dispersed worldwide, challenge the hold of custom on the lives of people. Second, the ability of technology to supplement human energies, both physical and mental, with machine power makes possible production of great quantities and varieties of cultural products. Third, the use of technology to expand production for the purpose of satisfying human wants depends on natural resources available and the development of economic structures suitable for exploitation of these resources. Fourth, within any society that has a reliable supply of natural resources, access to modern technical knowledge, and an effective economic system, the stage is set for rapid cultural change, including change in forms of dress. Section IV, therefore, is concerned with the relative effects of custom, technology, economic factors, and mobilized forces for change in the determination of dress in different types of societies and segments of societies.

In the last chapter we comment on similar problems that people encounter in covering and ornamenting their bodies. In addition, an appraisal is made of conditions that foster or deter movements toward world unity in form of dress. Some speculations are made on the future of dress.

Mary Ellen Roach
Joanne B. Eicher

I

the STUDY of DRESS

1

RECORDS
OF THE FORMS
OF DRESS

As we chronicle, summarize, and interpret the use of dress, we must first identify the forms of dress devised throughout the ages. Numerous resource materials are available to us: we learn about form from actual items of dress, written descriptions, and a wide variety of visual records, including painting and sculpture that show representations of dress.

actual artifacts

Study which depends on reference to actual artifacts is necessarily limited. Whereas items of contemporary dress are readily available, much from earlier eras has been destroyed or has deteriorated

Fig. 1–1. Among examples of artifacts associated with dress is a bone needle which was found in the state of Washington and believed to be 13,000 years old.

through time. Few garments dated earlier than the seventeenth century have survived. Jewelry, however, and other "hard" body equipment such as armor have sometimes been preserved from much earlier times. In fact, some items of body ornament, such as beads made of nonreactive minerals, have lasted for thousands of years and are identified among possessions of prehistoric man. On the other hand, the preservation of perishable organic materials, such as cottons, linens, silks, wools, leathers, and furs that have been used in apparel in various parts of the world for centuries, occurs only under unusual circumstances. Extreme cold, dryness, or a fortuitous combination of environmental conditions may sometimes forestall the deteriorating effects of oxygen, light, and micro-organisms and preserve clothing, or fragments of clothing, from earlier eras.

Undisturbed "cold storage" in the low temperatures of permanently frozen soil of northern Russia probably accounts for preservation of Old Stone Age leather and fur garments included among archeological finds reported by Russian scientists in the 1960s.[1] In one burial site the remains of two young boys were found clad in leather trousers and shirts and fur-lined boots. Beads of mammoth ivory decorated their apparel. In another grave a Cro-Magnon type man was buried in trousers and shirt of fur, also decorated with beads of mammoth ivory. Bracelets of mammoth ivory and strands of Arctic fox teeth added to his personal adornment.

In ancient burial sites in Egypt and the central Andean region of South America, clothing made of several types of fibers have resisted the devastations of time because of the dryness of the desert areas in which burials were made. Flax was the fiber used almost exclusively in the tunics, shawls, loin cloths, skirts, and robes recovered from Egyptian burials. However, the people of the Central Andes had more variety. Cotton; hair fibers from various animals, such as the vicuna, guanaco, and llama; and occasionally human hair and some bast fiber were used in the array of ponchos, skirts, shirts, breechclouts, shawls, turbans, and belts that have been retrieved from burial sites there.

Because of a chance favorable combination of burial arrangement and soil conditions, both the "hard" and the "soft" ware of dress have been found in remarkably good state of preservation in Scandinavian graves of the Bronze Age (1500–1100 B.C.).[2] In these oak coffin burial sites some of the oldest complete garments preserved from Western Europe have been discovered, along with pins, earrings, armrings, combs, and other ornaments of bronze. Cut and sewn jackets, and wraparound skirts, loin cloths, gowns, and cloaks

Fig. 1–2. Fragments of an eighteenth-century wool trade coat found near Bay City, Michigan. (Used with permission of the Michigan State University Museum.)

of woven wool were the basic garments. Men's hats were sometimes made in an intricate pile technique, women's caps by complicated braiding; shoes and sandals were of leather. Especially unique was a woman's thigh-length wraparound skirt made of cords twisted into a long fringe.

visual representations

For pictorial and other visual representations of dress we are indebted to many different kinds of craftsmen. In the twentieth century the visual record has been highly developed by photographers specializing in still photography, motion pictures, and television. For visual information previous to the second half of the nineteenth century, we are dependent mainly on the works of: painters, including the earliest caveman who practiced his art on the walls of his cave as well as his numerous descendants who have recorded their im-

Fig. 1–3. Cavemen practiced their art on the walls of their caves and recorded their impressions of human appearance. ("The White Lady of Aouanrhet," Tassili-n-Ajjer, Algeria. Courtesy of Henri Lhote's expedition.)

Fig. 1–4. Yoruba craftsmen recorded details of dress in Western Yorubaland on these wooden figures. (Used with the permission of Field Museum of Natural History.)

Fig. 1–5. Potters have fashioned vessels in human form. (Peruvian Mochica, "Strirrup Spout Head" headdress; rectangular, geometric pattern with step diagonals, circles, and triangles. 14″ [h] x 9½″ [w]. Buckingham fund. Courtesy of The Art Institute of Chicago.)

Fig. 1–6. Textiles can depict costume as in the case of this piece of embroidery. ("The Last Supper Textile." Courtesy of The Art Institute of Chicago.)

pressions of human appearance on various surfaces; sculptors who
have modeled recognizable human forms from clay, wood, ivory,
and rough chunks of stone; potters who have fashioned vessels in
human form or decorated them with human figures; metal workers
who have etched human figures on precious or base metals or cast
figures in metal; weavers, whose hands and tools have translated
threads of different color, size, and texture into pictures; engravers,
lithographers, and other printers who have made illustrations widely
available.

The contributions of the craftsmen who depended largely on the
skill of their hands are considerable and at times the only clues we

Fig. 1–7.   Portrait art like that of the eighteenth-century painter
John Singeleton Copley yields rich details about the appearance of
people of that time. (John Singleton Copley, "Mary Greene Hubbard,"
oil on canvas, 50⅜" x 39¹⁵⁄₁₆". Art Institute Purchase. Courtesy of
The Art Institute of Chicago.)

have to the nature of costume form and use in a particular era or place. Portrait art, depictions of historical events, and travelers' sketches yield some of the richest detail. A special contribution of the sixteenth century was the printing in Europe of costume plates depicting not only European, but also New World, Oriental, and African dress. These products of the engraver's art helped to satisfy an expanded desire for recording that came with the enthusiasm for exploration that blossomed in Western Europe at this time and set a pattern for the centuries to follow.

References in the Bible promoted early interest in and awareness of remote areas in Asia and Africa, but concepts of what these places were like and how people must have looked were, for most medieval Europeans, based on legends that had been handed down from classical times. Legend was blended with information from historians, particularly the Greek historian Herodotus who for his time had traveled rather widely in Asia Minor, Persia, the Mediterranean Islands, Egypt, and Lybia. Errors which he made in recording were perpetuated and compounded by later Roman historians, such as Solinus and Pliny who drew on him heavily for information, and sometimes added stories and legends of their own. Even as late as the end of the fifteenth century, the engravings of the Nuremberg Chronicles, which are one of the earliest products of the European printing press, reinforced classic misconceptions by representing inhabitants of remote regions of Asia or Africa as having grotesque and distorted bodies.

But minds were unlocked as information was brought back to Europe by fifteenth- and sixteenth-century explorers and travelers. Sketches of men, women, and children made in many parts of the world showed that human beings in far-off lands did not have the extreme physical deviations that had so long been imagined, although they might dress in unfamiliar ways, very different from the European, or scarcely cover their bodies at all. German engravings by Theodore DeBry, published in 1590 and 1591, are early examples of prints of costume from the New World. The unique dress of the Indians of Florida and Virginia depicted—the hairdresses, body painting and tattooing, and the generally bare bodies clad only incidentally in deerskin aprons or cloaks, sometimes a strap of interwoven moss—must have seemed exotic to the Europeans. DeBry's prints of Florida were taken from paintings done by Jacques LeMoyne Demorgues and are thought to have been done from memory after Demorgues returned to France from his travels in Florida in 1564 or 1565. His prints of Virginia are adapted from water colors done by John White who resided for awhile with the settlers in the Roanoke colonies established by Sir Walter Raleigh between

Fig. 1–8. John White's on-the-scene paintings of Indians around the Roanoke colonies, 1585–1587, are regarded as the earliest authentic pictorial records of aboriginal life in what is now the United States. ("The Flyer." Courtesy of the American Museum of Natural History.)

1585 and 1587.[3] Since White's paintings were on-the-scene records, they are regarded as the earliest authentic pictorial records of aboriginal life in what is now the United States.

Also important to our knowledge of costume are pictorial records that have been deliberately made in order to preserve knowledge of antiquity. For example, Francois Roger de Gaigniere's collection of sketches made between 1670–88 from art work on funerary and other monuments have been a much utilized source for redrawn illustrations used in books on early French costume.[4] Commissioned by Gaignieres to do the actual work was an artist-engraver Louis Bordeau. This work eventually passed into the hands of Louis XIV, and was finally deposited with the national archives of France, where it is still preserved.

Expanding mercantile interest in clothing, particularly in France, began to be noticeable as miniature representations of the newest ideas in women's fashions were sent from Paris on fashion dolls to centers of business throughout Europe, and even across the Atlantic to America. Use of these dolls is thought to date back to the late fourteenth century. In the seventeenth and eighteenth centuries they were a primary means for supplying the latest word in French fashion, including millinery, and, by the latter half of the eighteenth century, fashions in coiffures. The production of costume plates began about 1500, and became a well-developed art in the seventeenth century. By the end of the eighteenth century costume plates, which are after-the-fact portrayals of established mode, must be distinguished from fashion plates which, like the fashion dolls, were used to promote and publicize new fashions.[5] Early costume and fashion plates included depictions of men's dress; however, these diminished in importance by the late eighteenth century, as fashion competition among Western men began to wane, and fashion display became more the province of women. Women's fashion magazines

Fig. 1–9. Fashion plates like this *Godey's Ladies Book* example were used to promote and publicize new fashions but also became a visual record of dress. (Courtesy of Culver Pictures, Inc.)

and general women's magazines that carried fashion plates emerged at this time and were the forerunners of numerous publications of the nineteenth and twentieth centuries. Fashion plates were colored by hand until late in the nineteenth century when a general change to color printing took place.

The introduction of photography in the nineteenth century forewarned twentieth century Western fashion promotion via the work of the photographer rather than the artist or copyist, although sketches done in modern reproduction processes like offset-lithography are used in American pattern illustrations and sometimes in special art work. Costume history books, the evolutionary offspring of earlier collections of costume plates, have also moved to the utilization of photographs rather than drawings, although many costume history books still depend primarily on drawings for illustration. Davenport's monumental work published in the late 1940s depended for its illustrations on photographs of art work, and led the way for a growing number of "art books" on costume that have used improved methods of photography and printing, including color, for their depictions of costume.

The photographer cannot stray so far from actual appearance in recording pictures of dress as can the artist or copyist, yet neither the handcrafted plate nor the photograph can be guaranteed to mirror reality. Both may depict proposed fashions in dress rather than real modes of dress. Especially when conditions promote great social and economic inequalities, illustrations of dress tend to be characteristic of only those who have prestige and money; the dress of the poor, showing little variation in form, commands relatively little interest. A further distortion encouraged by publications on costume in the nineteenth and twentieth centuries is emphasis on women's dress and the downplaying of that of men. Interest in publishing pictures of men's dress waned as the dress of men of the nineteenth century became increasingly drab and standardized: the growing number of middle class businessmen devoted their time and energies to making money rather than to competing in fashion. However, the women in their families, wives and daughters, had the time to indulge in personal display. People with money rather than royalty began to lead fashion as the prestige of a leisured royalty lessened. A trend toward more variation and more rapid change in men's dress in the second half of the twentieth century may be a reflection of an increase in leisure time for a greater number of men, for time as well as money must be available if an individual is to take part in fashion changes. This move toward more participation in fashion

Fig. 1–10. Fashion photographs are records of dress. (Courtesy of *Vogue*, copyright 1969 by The Condé Nast Publications Inc.)

changes has been accompanied by an increased interest in fashion illustrations showing men's dress.

Many kinds of commercial artists other than the illustrators of fashion periodicals, depict dress in their paintings and drawings. For example, artists have been commissioned in many countries to paint or draw indigenous costumes for postage stamps.[6] Often times commercial artists incorporate dress in their advertisements for mass media. Frequently the costume is accurate and up-to-date, providing a true historical record. Other times aspects of dress are exaggerated or distorted in order to get a certain effect to increase sales appeal. Similar distortion can arise in portraiture, for artists frequently idealize their subjects. Their ability to depict reality may also be limited by art conventions or the media they use.

Whenever we start to show our age, we do a little face lifting.

When it rains, it pours.

Fig. 1-11. Commercial artists often depict dress in creating advertisements for mass media. (Courtesy of Morton Salt Company, A Division of Morton-Norwich Products, Inc.)

written description and commentary

Since artists may deviate from exact, visual representations, the accuracy of their pictures needs to be determined by cross-checking with other kinds of available data. One way to check is to consult written descriptions and commentaries on dress of the same time, when such material is available. Diaries, accounts of travel and exploration, catalogs, biographies, novels, memoirs, essays, satires, books of history and philosophy, manuals on etiquette and personal conduct, and religious tracts are often rich sources of information on dress, even when not primarily intended for this purpose. They can provide information to help validate the authenticity of visual representations and to elucidate the meaning of dress within its contemporary setting, although they, too, may be subject to bias. They can also contribute original information unavailable through visual media. Since essays, manuals on etiquette, and books on philosophy are highly interpretive, giving special points of view, their consideration will be reserved for Chapter Two.

Accounts of Travelers and Explorers

Travelers and explorers, sometimes intrigued and sometimes dismayed by customs that varied from their own, have provided us with many descriptions and comments on dress. Marco Polo's account of his thirteenth century travels in Medieval Asia was received with scepticism in his own day, when legend seemed more believable than the remarkable tales he told. Eventually accepted as an honest account, his book is an example of a volume that, in its rich description of customs, included information on dress, although references to elegant fabrics of silk and gold are more numerous than references to dress itself. His ill-concealed astonishment concerning dress of women in Balashan, a province north of Afghanistan, is reported in this way:

A peculiar fashion of dress prevails amongst the women of the superior class, who wear below their waists, in the manner of drawers, a kind of garment, in the making of which they employ, according to their means, an hundred, eighty, or sixty ells of fine cotton cloth; which they also gather or plait, in order to increase the apparent size of their hips; those being accounted the most handsome who are the most bulky in that part.[7]

Captain Cook's journal provided Europeans with some of the first detailed information on the general appearance and dress of peoples of the South Pacific little known even 250 years after Magellan's historic circumnavigating of the globe had opened the way. His account of tattooing as practiced in Tahiti, one of many stopping points on his journeys, is as follows:

Both sexes paint their bodys, tattow, as it is called in their Language. This is done by inlaying the Colour of Black under their skins in such a manner as to be indelible . . . Their method of Tattowing I shall now describe. The colour they use is lampblack prepar'd from the Smoak of a kind of Oily nut, used by them instead of Candles.[8]

An example of a more opinionated traveler, one who failed to endear herself to nineteenth century Americans because of her devastatingly candid observations of their personal habits, was Mrs. Trollope. Her book on the *Domestic Manners of Americans,* published in 1832, dwells on many fine details related to the grooming, dress, and appearance of Americans. Her attitude toward the accomplishments of Americans in this respect is well reflected in the following paragraph:

The ladies have strange ways of adding to their charms. They powder themselves immoderately, face, neck, and arms, with pulverized starch; the effect is indescribably disagreeable by day-light, and not very favourable at any time. They are also most unhappily partial to false hair, which they wear in surprising quantities; this is the more to be lamented, as they generally have very fine hair of their own. I suspect this fashion to arise from an indolent mode of making their toilet, and from accomplished ladies' maids not being very abundant; it is less trouble to append a bunch of waving curls here, there, and everywhere, than to keep their native tresses in perfect order.[9]

Costume History

In costume history visual representations and written commentary meet. Costume history volumes began with the binding together of collections of costume plates whose printing followed the introduction of the printing press. They took on added dimensions as descriptive texts were added. Books by Hope, Planche, Weiss, and Fairholt in the first half of the nineteenth century were forerunners of a number of books on European costume history that became popular in the last quarter of that century.[10] Among the best known of the latter were those by Quicherat, Racinet, Hottenroth, and Kretschmer and Rohrbach.[11] The twentieth century has witnessed an expanding interest in clothing customs, and many volumes on Western costume have been published. Increasing the knowledge of the Westerner of the history of non-Western costume are works such as Fabri's and Ghurye's individual volumes on Indian costume, Minnich's *Japanese Costume,* Wood and Osborne's *Indian Costumes of Guatemala,* Scott's *Chinese Costume in Transition,* Mead's *Traditional Maori Clothing,* Cordry's *Mexican Indian Costumes,* and Fairservis' *Costumes of the East.*[12]

One notable development in many twentieth century costume histories is an increased emphasis on examination and interpretation of costume within a total social, cultural, economic, and political context. Changes in form of costume are studied in relation to other changes in a society, instead of as isolated social phenomena, and viewpoints that arbitrarily classify forms as good or bad and changes as frivolous or socially undesirable are avoided. Among books on Western costume published since the mid-1940s, Davenport's *The Book of Costume* is one of the richest in explanatory detail.[13] Boucher's *A History of Costume* and Payne's *History of Costume* are further examples.[14] The previously mentioned books on non-Western costume also relate clothing to various factors that provide a backdrop for understanding human behavior.

summary

Dress has so fascinated man that he has long felt the urge to record its many forms; therefore, many sources of information are available to persons wishing to study the forms of dress throughout the ages. Sculpture, paintings, and ceramics provide visual representations from very ancient times; and pictorial textiles and printed plates showing dress, as well as actual costume artifacts, are available from about the sixteenth century. Supplementing information from visual representations and actual artifacts are accounts of travelers and explorers. Costume histories, which have flourished during the last two centuries, summarize data from many of these sources. Modern costume histories are made more exact through the use of photographs of actual objects, often in color.

2

WRITTEN INTERPRETATIONS OF DRESS

Prescriptive literature, philosophical treatises, moralistic essays, theoretical works, and research reports and reviews provide information and insights concerning the relation of dress to human needs and behavior. They help us understand why certain forms are preferred to others, for what purposes an individual uses dress, and what functions dress serves within society.

moralistic essays, satire, and reform literature

Writers through the ages have made form of dress a matter of morals and have recorded their approval or disapproval of different forms of dress on moral grounds. As they have done so, they have revealed some of the meaning of dress in their time. Although the form of moralistic attacks often has the ring of ritualistic consistency, philosophical bases for moralizing may be quite different. Thus the ardent sixteenth century Puritan, Philip Stubs, sets forth arguments against the dress of his day that sound very much like those of Clay Geerdes, a contributor to an underground newspaper of the 1960s.

Stubs said in 1595:

For doe not the most of our . . . newfangled fashions rather deforme, then adorne us: disguise us, then become us: making us rather to resemble savage beastes and brutish Monsters, then continent, sober and chast Christians.[1]

Geerdes said in 1969:

Cosmetics do not make women beautiful, they symbolize artificiality and unnatural image which are truly ugly masks of people unable to accept themselves as they really are.[2]

One roots his arguments in religious doctrine, the other in popular psychology.

Fig. 2–1. Cartoons are a type of literary and visual satire and frequently use current fashion for subject matter. (Cartoon by Dave Gerard. Reprinted courtesy of *Parade* Magazine.)

D. GERARD

"You mean he isn't anybody and he dresses like that?"

The symbolic nature of dress encourages the satirist, as moralist, to use dress as a symbol of man's follies and vices that he would like to expose. Thus *clothes* are the vehicle for exposition, rather than the target of nineteenth century philosophizing, in Carlyle's *Sartor Resartus* (originally titled "Thoughts on Clothes"). Nevertheless, what he has to say reveals how dress is similar to other social inventions and how it can become an integral part of the social fabric of mankind:

> *Clothes, from the King's mantle downwards, are emblematic, not of want only, but of a manifold cunning Victory over Want. On the other hand, all emblematic things are properly Clothes, thought-woven. . . . Men are properly said to be clothed with Authority, clothed with Beauty, with Curses, and the like.*[3]

Special forms of satire are cartoon and caricature; they capture the basic elements of a current fashion and make them explicit through exaggeration. These two forms of satire also use dress to symbolize specific individuals or types of individuals.

prescriptive literature

Customs, or standard modes of behavior, emerge in a society whenever it has existed long enough for people to recognize the economy of the ritualized act that will help a person cope with regularly occurring events with a minimum expenditure of energy. In countries with strong inclinations toward class distinctions, standards for appearance may serve to support social differences. They can make clear to all that one in the lower classes does not ape his betters, but dresses according to his "station in life," and that one in the "better classes" does not sanction freedom in dress of his inferiors lest it lead to uncontrollable or disagreeable insubordination.

Prescriptive literature on dress describes some of the customs in dress that have helped people get along with each other in the past. They are, therefore, presented as ways of guaranteeing success in social relations in the present and future. In America, prescriptive standards for insuring success in presentation of one's appearance have been abundant in newspapers, magazines, books and manuals on clothing selection and dress, and in general manuals for proper behavior or etiquette. In the nineteenth century general manuals on etiquette were ordinarily much concerned with dress and sometimes used subtitles to so indicate. They found a rich soil for survival in America, a country that has sheltered people torn from many different traditional ways and forced to work together in a joint effort to create a new life that would promote both individual and common good. A vast majority of the early immigrants were unencumbered by knowledge of "right" modes of personal behavior for the "best society" since they themselves were derived from the lower classes. Moreover, no hereditary aristocracy that could serve as example for behavior existed in the land they came to. However, busy as they were with hewing a place for themselves out of the wilderness, they longed for some cultivation in the social graces that would somehow enhance the quality of American life. That a hunger for knowing how to behave properly existed in early decades of the nineteenth century is clear, since magazines such as *Godey's Lady's Book* include many suggestions on etiquette and dress, and since there was a great demand for manuals devoted to social decorum. Schlesinger comments:

From the late 1820s on, this literature poured forth in a never-ending stream. An incomplete enumeration shows that, aside from frequent revisions and new editions, twenty-eight different manuals appeared in the late 1850s—an average of over three new ones annually in the pre-Civil War decades.[4]

Americans felt self-conscious about their manners and dress as they compared themselves with self-confident Europeans, particularly the French and English. Thus, Mrs. Duffey in 1876 urged her countrymen to cast off their feelings of inferiority and dependency and strike off for themselves to develop an American style of behavior. She presented her case in this way:

We have so long borrowed our manners, like our literature, from the Old World, that we have become thoroughly imbued with the feeling that what is not European—what is not at least English—cannot be proper and right in the conduct of life. But now, in the hundredth year of our national existence, it is time we began to realize the fact that we are perfectly capable of depending upon ourselves in matters pertaining to both behavior and dress. Our civilization is American; and, all unaware of it as we are, our development of the finer and gentler traits of character is just as truly American. We should understand that the American gentleman, though he may be lacking in the exceedingly polished, almost subservient, outward forms of politeness of the Frenchman—though he may not be so self-asserting and condescending as the Englishman—is just as true a gentleman; and the type which he presents would be more acceptable to the American People. Under-

neath an occasional appearance of brusqueness is hidden an even greater respect for women—that touchstone of true gentility. Our national institutions themselves teach men to respect one another as those of no nation do.

There is an unwritten code of manners in our best American society, and there is no better code on the face of the earth. . . .[5]

But deference to the English and French was hard to stifle. It showed up in the 1920's as Emily Post admonished men on how to dress properly. She said:

If you would dress like a gentleman, you must do one of two things, either study the subject of a gentleman's wardrobe until you are competent to pick out good suits from freaks, or buy only English ones. It is not Anglomania, but plain common sense to admit that, just as the Rue de la Paix in Paris is the fountainhead of fashions for women, Bond Street in London is the home of irreproachable clothes for men.[6]

And the English, as well as the Americans, could bow to the French in matters of women's dress. Mrs. Merrifield, an English woman in the mid-nineteenth century, complained about the influence of French fashion on the English, yet she succumbed to its power as she sprinkled her writing with French fashion terms and finally admitted a superior talent among the French by saying:

The French, whose taste in dress is so far in advance of our own, say that ladies who are cinquante ans sonnes (on the wrong side of fifty), should neither wear gay colours, nor dress of slight materials, flowers, feathers, or much jewelry; that they should cover their hair, wear high dresses, and long sleeves.[7]

To the extent that nineteenth-century American manuals on decorum were aimed at a common behavior suitable for all social levels, they facilitated the geographical and social mobility of dwellers in a newly adopted land. However, Schlesinger points out that the rise of a new group of moneyed people following the Civil War encouraged a lingering deference to a code of social differences. People who made fortunes overnight in such areas as mining, railroads, banking, and real estate yearned after a style of life appropriate to their newly elevated status. To provide for their needs, manuals on decorum were written that explained ways for developing more aristocratic behavior. These manuals thereby helped perpetuate belief in a well-ordered society based on individuals learning behavior appropriate to their stations in life and beyond which they should not aspire. To do so was at the risk of unknown perils, if one is to believe an exhortation from a popular book of the day. It warned:

Never dress above your station; it is a grevious (sic) mistake, and leads to great evils, besides being the proof of an utter want of taste.[8]

With the readjustments in society following World War I, the day of the conspicuous consumption of the *nouveau riche* who had dominated American society in the latter part of the nineteenth century and early part of the twentieth century, was over and references to matters of adjusting one's appearance to indicate his station in life disappeared from even the more formal and tremendously popular etiquette manuals of Lillian Eichler and Emily Post.[9] In addition, a new type of book aimed clearly at the masses instead of the leisured well-to-do appeared and was frankly aimed toward making getting along with one's fellow as easy as possible. One of these books, intended to produce instant etiquette for the harried masses, began with this forthright introduction:

The tempo of our times demands an etiquette book designed for instantaneous reference. The Common Sense Etiquette Dictionary *satisfies a definite and an urgent need. It contains—without padding, sermonizing or moralizing—the essentials for good-breeding. It gives a bird's eye view of the entire field of manners—all one needs to know to move gracefully, confidently, and easily among his fellows. All non-essentials have been eliminated.*

Etiquette is in a continual state of flux. A last year's etiquette book is more or less outmoded. Time waits for no man. Neither does etiquette. Manners move on.[10]

Like general manuals on etiquette, twentieth-century books devoted specifically to the art of dress or the selection of clothing have moved away from moralizing to suggestions for dress that will facilitate social relations at the same time that they allow some personal satisfactions in the aesthetic affect of dress. Since these books offer only one society's set of solutions to the art of dress, they are not necessarily applicable within another. Sometimes they are applicable only within a segment of a society. They fall into the prescriptive category as they propose to delineate the *best* ways in which an individual can dress in order to appear handsome, beautiful (or some approximation thereof), and in order to feel socially at ease in various places and on different occasions. For example, Grace Morton's long established book on selection of women's clothing states ideal appearance very exactly, and gives very specific directions for "making" a face approach the most acceptable appearance. It states:

In silhouette the ideally shaped face is an ovoid, slightly flattened at the sides. The widest part of the face should come between the cheekbones, and the width should be approximately three-fourths the length of the face. . . .

The square face . . . needs to be made longer and less wide. There is the additional problem of reducing the angularity in the square face. Essentially vertical line movement with a transitional element is needed. The shapes of details likewise should be transitional without sharp angles or full roundness. The jewel and bateau necklines, chokers, and earrings are to be avoided.[11]

In a book titled *Clothing Selection*, Chambers and Moulton also prescribe as they describe properties of men's dress:

In a properly fitted suit, where a turtleneck sweater, a scarf, or a Nehru shirt is worn, the height of the neckline should flatter the individual. (1) the collar should set low enough to show about one-half an inch of the shirt collar. It should be a comfortable but snug fit; (2) the shoulders of the suit should ride easily on the individual's shoulders, but remain in place. Both shoulders of the suit should be the same height and width; (3) lapels, if properly constructed, remain close and smooth against the chest.[12]

The posture of the writer of prescriptive literature on dress is recognizable by the "shoulds" and "should nots," by the "dos" and the "don'ts," implied or real, proffered to the reader. Suggestions for dress are stated more as unchallengable premises than as social variables. However, the enduring quality of any rules for personal behavior is sorely tried in a rapidly changing society such as in America where recommended social usages run the risk of being obsolete before a book ever reaches its publication date. On the other hand, the persistence of some themes for proper dress through decades, as documented by some of the American published books on the art or etiquette of dress, reveals the stability of culture. The rightness and wrongness of human size, for example, cannot be measured by a fixed metric that applies to all societies and to all eras. However, in books on women's dress dated 1854, 1941, and 1969, suggestions have been made for how to dress to correct for "wrong" height.[13] What proper height may be is not always expressed in feet or inches; but the reader, immersed in the folkways of her own society, can be expected to be aware of the approximate measures for what is too tall and too short. The American woman will sense that height has something to do with her personal attractiveness, probably her marriageability and may, therefore, seek suggestions for some socially acceptable ways of dressing to direct attention away from her discrepancy from a socially felt desirable range in height.

Books on etiquette and manuals on how to dress have continued as items of popular consumption in the United States in the latter half of the twentieth century; many titles are always in print. However, they are usually published for the benefit of women. Men's nineteenth century withdrawal from fashion competition is reflected in selection books as well as costume history books—books devoted to selecting men's clothes are very few in number compared to similar books for women. A 1939 volume, *Men Too Wear Clothes*, notes the difference between attention given the sexes in its title.[14] Depending on the discretion with which they are used, prescriptive works can act as democratic, socializing agents preparing individuals for social interaction and acceptance in social groups they are unacquainted with. Their feelings of self-confidence may be enhanced to the extent that prescribed dress facilitates their acceptance among social groups of importance to them. However, the mobile person has no assurance that an author's recommendations for dress will fit all situations in all locales, even in the United States, since pluralistic sentiments encourage local differences and each author speaks from the bias of his own background. The region an author comes from makes a difference in his perspective, as does his being male or female, old or young, rich or poor, black or white. Particularly in matters of appropriateness for different occasions, an author's recommendations have to be tested and checked "on location," since they may not fit. Take for example the term "informal dress." In the 1970s this can be interpreted as anything from fine dress, just short of what is locally thought the most formal, to the very least formal, blue jeans and sneakers. Who is defining makes the difference.

In addition, books on etiquette and proper dress run the risk of being quickly outdated by swiftly changing fashions. They almost always are a look backward to a society's most suitable requirements for personal behavior and may, therefore, leave out peripheral matters that nevertheless stimulate great social discomfort. If they describe much specific detail such as colors, widths, lengths, types of collars and cuffs, they almost inevitably take on the quaint quality of bygone days by the time of publication.

Since these books reflect ideal patterns for human contacts on a person-to-person basis, they preserve an intimate view of life in a particular time. The view may be from a particular bias or angle and may describe the ideal act that is seldom executed in reality. But the aspirations of a people, no matter how effectively they are put to practice, have a reality of their own—they are powerful influences on the directions for all kinds of behavior. Also a codification of ideal behavior that represents majority inclination rather than social consensus can never be completely acceptable to all people within a society. That some will always be left out of the range of the desirable in appearance can provoke resentment and anger and invite questioning of the social justice of unattainable ideals. The ancient cliche that "you can't judge a book by its cover" expresses protest against prescription.

At the same time, prescribed forms of dress contribute to orderly behavior because they reduce interpretations of appearances to a comprehensible number and encourage rapport. People do not have to go through a lengthy getting-acquainted process in order to establish some basis for communication. In business, this kind of conservation of time may be especially useful. Knowing the sales person in a store at a glance from his dress speeds the business transaction on its way.

On a more personal basis, books on clothing selection and dress offer individuals an opportunity to learn the aesthetic tools and standards of his own culture and something about the aesthetic limits within which he can express himself and still feel appreciated and somehow self-fulfilled within his own society. Twentieth-century clothing selection books that make suggestions for "how to buy" reflect America's shift to mass-produced clothes of many kinds in vast quantity. Learning to evaluate how materials and manufacturing techniques affect achieving the kind of aesthetic effect one desires is often stressed. In addition, suggestions are often made on how to choose among alternative items, with money available, and still arrive at an appearance that satisfies current ideals.

analytical works

Written interpretations that stress understanding of dress, rather than reform or preservation of prescribed forms of dress are recent in man's history. That costume history moved in this direction has already been noted in Chapter One. The roots for this change and the expansion of behavioral studies related to dress lay within an early interest of social scientists in the phenomenon.

As scholars in the various rudimentary social sciences were probing all kinds of human behavior, many focused part of their attention on dress and fashion. Certain conditions encouraged this interest. First of all, in the second half of the nineteenth century the Women's Dress Reform Movement, an arm of the Women's Rights Movement, made women's dress a social issue. Ridiculed severely and frustrated in their efforts when led by Mrs. Bloomer and her successors to introduce trousers and other kinds of reform dress, those active in the dress reform movement would never have dreamed of the drastic changes that finally came with general social shifts in the 1920s.

Fig. 2–2. Amelia Bloomer was among those responsible for interest in initiating different forms of dress for women. (Courtesy of Culver Pictures, Inc.)

Secondly, interest was aroused concerning fashion, as fashion changes, especially in women's clothing, were taking place more and more rapidly. These rapid changes occurred as nineteenth-century industrialization resulted in development of means for producing new fashions quickly and inexpensively. Unraveling the mysteries of the evolving fashion system that reached out both nationally and internationally became a challenge. Social psychologists, inspired by works of Tarde and Le Bon,[15] were especially interested in what generates collective changes in behavior subject to fashion influence; however, economists also included fashion in their realm of concern.

The relation of clothing to sexual experience and interplay represented a third focus of interest. This interest was given expression as scientific treatises on sex broke the publication barrier, sometimes with great difficulty.

Although many of the writings of the social scientists are in the form of short journal articles, somewhat difficult to summarize on a broad scale, a fairly clear picture of social science developments in the study of dress can be drawn by consulting published books and monographs. Therefore, the rest of this chapter is devoted, with rare exception, to a summary of the latter kinds of works.

Krafft-Ebing's *Psychopathia Sexualis* (1886), Freud's *The Interpretation of Dreams* (1900), and Havelock Ellis's *Studies in the Psychology of Sex* (c. 1901) (the latter published after great controversy) opened a new era of open scientific discussion of sexuality.[16] All of these works made some reference to aspects of clothing or appearance. In Krafft-Ebing's case studies attention was called to transvestism and the sexual symbolism of articles of clothing used as fetishes. The integration of clothing into the total complex of conscious and unconscious behavior was uncovered in Freud's analysis of the material of dreams. Both in *The Interpretation of Dreams* and later work he referred to the symbolism of dress.[17]

In *Studies in the Psychology of Sex,* heavily documented with cross-cultural and within culture references, Ellis treated a number of topics related to dress, or undress, in a manner formerly taboo. Modesty, nudity practices, clothing fetishes, and bodily enhancements such as perfumes and bathing were analyzed in their relation to human sexual behavior. Other works that followed, such as Thomas' *Sex and Society* (1907), also treated the subject of sexual behavior and clothes.[18]

Ross' *Social Psychology* (1908), on the other hand, showed great concern with the contagions of collective behavior that result in group action.[19] Thus the crowd, the mob, and fashion were subjects for his attention. German sociologist Simmel was also concerned with fashion.[20] Both he and Ross utilized theoretical concepts that had much in common with earlier theories of collective behavior presented by Tarde and Le Bon.

Veblen (1899), as an economist and social observer, maintained in his *The Theory of the Leisure Class* that dress symbolized the position of the leisured class.[21] Webb's *Heritage of Dress* (1907) was both within and without the mainstream of social science of his day.[22] His presentation was heavily weighted with traditional description of historical costume detail, but he also applied findings of psychologists in attempting to understand the effect of clothing on the individual and contributed an analysis of cultural survivals in dress.

Out of this incubation period early in the twentieth century, the first really comprehensive statement on dress came from an anthropologist, Crawley, and was published in the *Encyclopaedia of Religion and Ethics* (1912).[23] During the rest of this decade and the next, significant publications were few. An exception was Dearborn's 1918 monograph titled "Psychology of Clothing," which was unique because it looked at clothing in relation to the total behaving person.[24] It included lengthy discussion of the effects of clothing on physiological processes as well as upon social behavior and individual attitudes and behavior. However, not until the 1940s and thereafter were further reports of consequence published on the relation of clothing to physiology. In his *Physiology of Heat Regulation and the Science of Clothing* (1949), Newburgh presented many findings from studies by United States governmental agencies that had considered problems in design of protective clothing for survival in arctic regions, the tropics, high altitudes, and space.[25]

A later publication, *Clothing: Comfort and Function* by Fourt and Hollies (1970), emphasized the bio-physics of clothing.[26] More comprehensive than other publications on clothing and body physiology was Renbourn's *Materials and Clothing in Health and Disease* (1972), which touched on functions of materials and clothing and the psychology of dress as well as clothing and physiology.[27] Publications by anthropologists concerned with both human physical adaptation and cultural adaptation to environment have complemented these works.[28]

In the late twenties and the thirties came an upsurge of interest in publications on the psychological, social, and cultural implications of dress. This interest no doubt was associated with general sharp breaks with tradition at that time, symbolized so well in the dress of women: a women's leg fully exposed to the knee was a phenomenon unknown in polite Western society since the Greeks. Social scientists set to work to interpret what the implications of this and other drastic changes in dress were.

Hiler's *From Nudity to Raiment* (1929), written by an artist who developed a consuming desire to study dress, piqued interest as he probed existing literature for theories on origins of dress.[29] About the same time, two books on the psychology of clothing were published: Hurlock's *Psychology of Dress* and Flugel's very influential, psychoanalytically oriented book, *The Psychology of Clothes.*[30] In addition, Nystrom presented his *Economics of Fashion.*[31]

In the *Encyclopaedia of the Social Sciences,* published in 1931, were classic statements on dress, ornament, and fashion by anthropologists Benedict, Bunzel, and Sapir.[32] In the same year Crawley's 1912 essay was reprinted in a book with the ear-catching title *Dress, Drinks, and Drums.*[33] The introduction to Hiler and Hiler's 1939 *Bibliography of Costume* rivaled Crawley's work in its comprehensiveness.[34]

The decade of the thirties also stimulated the compilers of bibliography. Colas' bibliography appeared in 1933, the Monro and Cook *Costume Index* in 1937, and the previously mentioned Hiler and Hiler work in 1933.[35] These bibliographies followed by more than 30 years the only previous comprehensive index of costume, the catalog of the Lipperheide library that had classified more than 5,000 titles between 1896 and 1905.[36]

World War II depressed publication during the 1940s. Among volumes that did appear were Cunnington's *Why Women Wear Clothes,* which drew on social science theories and referred to the necessity for considering psychological factors in the understanding of dress; and *On Human Finery* by Bell who applied and expanded Veblen's concepts in analysis of dress.[37] Books in a light vein but reflecting social sensitivity were published by Elizabeth Hawes and Rudofsky.[38] Sheldon's *Varieties of Human Physique* and *Varieties of Temperament* presented materials closely related to dress since they dealt with aspects of personal appearance, in this case, types of body build.[39]

The 1950s saw influences of psychoanalytic concepts in several works. Laver, frequent contributor to costume history, confessed in his autobiography to plunging into "the muddy waters of psychoanalysis." One result was his adoption of Flugel's concept of shifting erogenous zones as partly explanatory of fashion change.[40] Bergler utilized the same theory in his *Fashion and the Unconscious,* as he formulated a systematic theoretical scheme for understanding dress.[41] His scheme, grounded in psychoanalytic theory, explained that the compulsions of fashion, like other behavior, evolve from conflict motives. In *The Importance of Wearing Clothes* Langner referred to Adler's refinements on psychoanalytic theory, notably his concepts of *inferiority* and *superiority,* as explanatory of dress.[42] These concepts were similar in idea to Laver's *hierarchial principle* expanded in his book *Clothes* (1952) and subsequent publications such as *Modesty in Dress,* published in 1969.[43] In proposing a hierarchial principle of dress Laver saw dress as a means of enhancing the owner's sense of importance. He rounded out his motivational triad by adding a *seduction principle* and a *utility principle.* His seduction principle emphasized that individuals may use dress to make themselves more desirable in the eyes of the opposite sex. The utility principle takes over for people who want items of dress that make their bodies more comfortable.

In the 1960s Stone's theoretical work "Appearance and the Self" presented an interactional framework for understanding dress.[44] It emphasized environmental rather than inborn influences on dress and thus differed from the 1950 works of psychoanalytic orientation. Such perspective was in general harmonious with a number of publications of the 1960s and 1970s. These works, typically eclectic in orientation, have applied research and theory from various social sciences in analyses of dress. Most of them have been presented as textbooks and each has its unique emphasis. Roach and Eicher's work, *Dress, Adornment, and the Social Order* which presented a collection of readings, emphasized understanding dress within a sociocultural context.[45] Ryan's book, *Clothing, a Study in Human Behavior,* was mainly a summary of research, and attempted to coordinate findings based on many different theoretical premises and to classify these according to their general social psychological significance.[46] Anspach, taking fashion as focus, in *The Why of Fashion* emphasized an economic viewpoint that regards clothing as a commodity.[47] However, clothing was viewed not only as an economic but also as a social and psychological phenomenon. Horn's work, *The Second Skin,* encompassed economic, social, and psychological viewpoints from the social sciences.[48] Points of view from aesthetics, as well as biological and physical sciences were incorporated. In an essay entitled "Fashion," Blumer has contributed a theory of fashion appropriate to contemporary mass society.[49] He sees the fashion system as a complex means for facilitating orderly change within a mass society no longer able to provide identity and maintain order via social custom. In *Collective Search for Identity,* Klapp directed his writing to a number of matters other than dress; however, he gave considerable attention to the problem of finding identity in mass society by proposing several means whereby a person may try to express his individuality through dress.[50] Three major concepts, awareness, symbols, and role were used by Rosencranz to analyze dress in her book, *Clothing Concepts: A Social Psychological Approach.*[51]

European publications since 1950 have also contributed to the sociological approach to the study of dress. These include publications by König and Brenninkmeyer.[52]

A special word should be said about anthropological monographs. Much informative material can be found in these sources and the searching through them can bear rich rewards. Since many monographs encompass the total life pattern of a people, clothing use and technology are often included. Monographs devoted exclusively to dress are rather rare; however, a few can be cited. Already mentioned is a study by Mead, a Maori looking at cultural traits within his own society.[53] The Stratherns' work, *Self-Decoration in Mount Hagan,* which focused on dress in the New Guinea Highland, is another.[54] Yet another is Bogatyrev's 1937 monograph, *Functions of Folk Costume in Moravian Slovakia,* recently translated into English.[55] Anthropological as well as other references have been collected in Eicher's *African Dress: A Select and Annotated Bibliography of Subsaharan Countries.*[56]

summary

Writers throughout history have revealed to us how the form of dress has been regarded by the people of their time. Contemporary writers describe the form of dress as right or wrong, moral or immoral, just as writers of a hundred or a thousand years ago did. A common American phenomenon of the nineteenth and twentieth centuries has been the writing of prescriptive articles and books that have defined dress customs and prescribed appropriate dress. Many of these American customs have been borrowed from others, particularly the English and French.

Works that have approached objective, unbiased analyses of dress and a search for understanding, rather than preservation of social custom, are mainly a product of the twentieth century. Contributors have been from many fields, including psychology, cultural anthropology, sociology, economics, and interdisciplinary fields such as home economics.

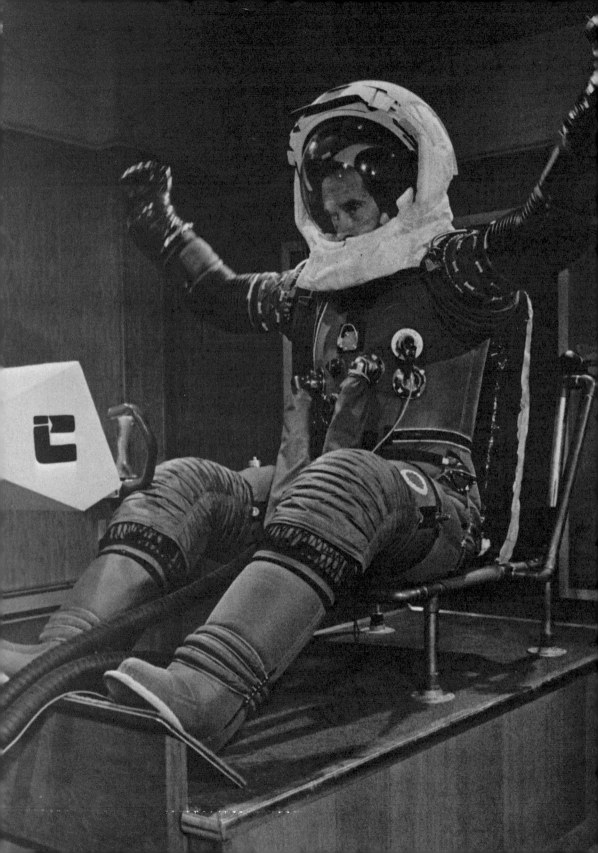

II

BODY
and DRESS

3

PHYSICAL APPEARANCE AND DRESS

Since the body is always a part of the total appearance a person presents, and coverings and adornment are necessarily designed in relation to the body, dress cannot be considered without also considering the physical characteristics of the body. These characteristics include general body contour (commonly called body build), facial features, amount of hair, hair texture and color, skin texture and color. First we shall consider the similarities among humans in physical appearance and then the differences. In addition, relations between dress and physical appearance will be noted.

similarities in physical characteristics

As *Homo sapiens,* all members of mankind display a great deal of similarity in physical characteristics. Schusky and Culbert point out that compared with other animal species, the degree of homogeneity within mankind is remarkable, for animal species similarly distributed in widely separated and greatly different environments have become differentiated into a number of distinct species.[1] All human beings, by way of contrast, are of a single species. This difference between man and other animals is attributed to man's ability to develop cultural adaptations that have allowed him a mobility impossible for other animal species. Man has a complex brain and nervous system coupled with a capacity for speech that enables him to develop and manipulate symbols. Man also has upright posture which frees his forearms from being used for locomotion. His freed forearms, and his opposable thumb, that enhance his grasping ability, allow him to be a tool-making and tool-using animal. Thus all human beings are capable of making artifacts to clothe and decorate their bodies and to develop a system of symbols connected with the items of dress. Man's capacity for cultural adaptation has made possible his migration into far parts of the world aided by body coverings, sheltering structures, heating and other temperature control systems that he has devised. Relationships among these various means for adapting to surroundings are referred to again in Chapter Four.

variations in physical characteristics

Variations in physical characteristics in man are related to the interplay of a number of factors, including environmental influences, heredity, and age.

Environmental Influences

When populations live in different natural environments without many cultural aids, different physical characteristics are likely to develop. Apparently those individuals with certain types of physical characteristics can survive in a particular environment while those with other characteristics cannot, thus a natural selection process eliminates the most unfit. Over a long period of time a fairly homogeneous type evolves that is suited for survival in the specific locale. Because different environments are likely to favor different kinds of physical characteristics for survival, a world-wide diversification of physical types occurs.

GEOGRAPH-
ICAL
BARRIERS

Diversification of groups of people is encouraged by geographical barriers such as deserts, oceans, and mountains; and social barriers such as language, religion, and political differences for these barriers prevent or retard the homogenizing effect of interbreeding. As geographic distance increases, physical differences between groups of people increase. Four groups, the Australoid, the Caucasoid, the Mongoloid, and the Negroid, in a general way, were historically separated from each other by physical barriers. These groups are often called *races,* a term that has many shortcomings because of the tendency to apply social prejudice in comparing one racial division with another.

In actuality, no clear-cut divisions of mankind have ever been made, nor is any likely to be made, since more and more mixing of populations is taking place. At best, races are categories that can be used to identify people on a crude basis as being "more like" or less like one race than another, or as having characteristics of several different races. The failure of racial types as a means of classifying people can be noted in studies of Pacific Islands: some groups remain unclassifiable and must be studied as distinct populations.

TECHNOLOGY

Tools, weapons, and machines, products of the technology of a people, are as influential a part of environment as climatic conditions, terrain, and natural barriers. In fact, the isolating effects of natural environment are often modified by the introduction of man-made tools and machines that facilitate movement from one place to another. In addition, some inventions have favored survival of people with specific body characteristics. The person most likely to survive is the one whose body allows him to be most skillful in handling the tools and weapons his culture provides.

Brues hypothesizes that in a technically undeveloped group that uses heavy clubs for defense, or in procuring animals for food, a heavily muscled body that can exert force will probably be the one best equipped for survival.[2] By way of contrast, people who have developed some type of hand-thrown projectile, such as a spear for hunting and defense, would be impeded by body bulk. They need for defense, and therefore survival, the kind of speed leverage for the *thrust* of the spear that is provided by a long forearm and a rangy body that enhances running ability. In the use of the bow, on the other hand, the source of energy is almost exclusively in the arms of the bowman. Therefore, the bowman needs the power leverage of short forearms supported by well-muscled broad shoulders. When man develops agriculture, he needs a body type more like that of the club bearer, for he has to work with heavy digging instruments to till the soil. Therefore, the agriculturist who can best survive is the one with a compact, heavy body that can apply direct force.

Not enough time has passed for us to know for sure how mechanization that replaces human physical energy, as in the present era, will affect evolution of body form. However, we can speculate on the basis of what appears to be happening. First of all, we can predict that the continued application of technology that provides much occupational diversity, as compared with the nontechnical society, will allow coexistence of many body forms. A standard type of body will not be necessary for dealing with standard problems of basic survival since hazards of the environment can be controlled or countered without the necessity of a physically skilled body adept at wielding a club, a spear, or other implement. In the mechanized society, tools are operated by the application of other than the physical power of the body. Both food production and the handling of weaponry are more matters of the application of mental than body skill.

NUTRITION AND DISEASE Both the amount and kind of food available may account for differences in body development. All people require the same nutrients in different amounts according to their age, sex, activities, size, and state of health. However, they may not have access to everything they need. Climate, for example, can limit what food can be grown. In the arctic region, where plant and animal life are limited by severe cold, the seal was long a major source of food for the Eskimo who needed a diet high in calories, such as seal fat gives, to make up for heat loss. In areas of heavy rainfall, such as southeast Asia, rice that can flourish in the water-soaked ground is an important food. Wheat and potatoes give a supply of nutrients for people in still other climates. In addition to climate, technology also affects food supply. Domestication of plants and animals allows control of food supply impossible among hunters and gatherers. Inedibles can sometimes be made edible if a suitable technology is developed. Thus poisonous bitter cassava can be converted into an important source of food starch in tropical regions of South America, Africa, and the Malaysian archipelago.

Once ways of preserving and transporting foods from place to place have been developed, climate may place fewer restrictions on food supply, for technology overcomes the restrictions. However, traditions that determine what is good or proper to eat may still limit nutrition. For instance, long-time habits and religious beliefs may prohibit use of some potentially nutritious foods by human beings.

If deprivation or imbalance of nutrients occurs, physical appearance may deviate from that of the well-nourished body in a number of ways: height and weight may be affected, bodies may swell, muscles may atrophy, skin and hair may change in color and texture, bones may be deformed, teeth may decay. Similar changes may also occur with many kinds of body malfunctions and disease.

Obesity is related to nutrition and health, but also to ideals of beauty. Obesity places strain on body organs, but may in some societies be felt aesthetically desirable. If obesity is considered beautiful, it may be encouraged and the matter of health disregarded. If nutrition and disease alter appearance, individuals may make changes in their dress and ornamentation. For example, they may endeavor to make adjustments in size or try to conceal effects of disease.

Heredity

Since the mechanisms of heredity are not fully understood, determining which body characteristics are strictly controlled by heredity and which by environment is not always possible. However, sex differentiation, and surface features such as hair color and form, eye color and form, and basic skin color, appear to be controlled by heredity, while general body shape and size, although dependent on heredity, appear to be greatly influenced by climate and diet. What is inherited by offspring will depend upon the mixing of genes from parents who carry genes for different inheritable physical characteristics, mutations that alter the traits that can be inherited, and the natural selection processes encouraged by physical or social environment.

SEX DIFFER-
ENTIATION
Beyond the obvious differences in sex organs, sex differentiations in appearance of body form are not as clear-cut as we are often led to believe. "Instead of fitting the stereotype for 'man' or 'woman,' each individual falls somewhere on a continuum running from almost 'all male' to almost 'all female' in physical characteristics." [3] In some populations, differences between male and female body configuration appear to be greater than others. Within any population, women are expected to be broader in the hips and narrower in the shoulders than men, but many exceptions occur. Greater pelvic width and development of breasts are probably the most consistently different secondary characteristics.

Fig. 3–1.   Clothing may emphasize or de-emphasize the female body.

Another generalization about humans is that the male tends to have more hair than the female. Men are more frequently able to grow beards and have hair on their legs, chests, stomachs, backs, and arms, as well as [around] their genitals. Women usually cannot grow beards, have almost no hair on their chests, stomachs, or back, and compared with men, have only light growths on their legs and arms.[4]

The physical differences between the sexes can be important in the type of clothing the sexes wear. Sometimes a society may emphasize sexual characteristics, at other times it may de-emphasize them. For example, a woman's costume with a tight waist reveals breast size

Fig. 3–2. Tunics de-emphasize male/female differences of body.

and shape and makes hips appear broad by contrast. On the other hand a loose, hip-length tunic worn over trousers will camouflage sexual characteristics, for both males and females.

SKIN   Skin color varies between human populations and within populations.[5] Isolation encourages homogeneity while social contacts among people of different skin colors encourage within-group variation. Skin colors vary from very light to very dark with a high proportion being tones of brown. All skins derive color from the pinkness of blood vessels below the surface of the skin and from pigments called melanins that are found in both light and dark skins. Melanin formation may result from exposure to the sun or may be genetic in origin. In some people the genetic ability to form melanin in the skin *without exposure* to the sun varies; in addition, people have different capacities for melanin formation in their skin *on exposure* to sunlight. A very light skin will derive most of its coloration from the capillaries below the surface of the skin but will still have some melanin pigments. The albino, who has no pigment in his skin, hair, or iris of the eyes, is the only exception. Albinos are rare but can occur in any population.

Melanins are in heavier concentration in dark skin than light skin. Since dark skin is more common in the hot areas of the world, some scientists think that it is an adaptive characteristic resulting from natural selection. They maintain that the dark skin filters out excessive ultra violet rays and thus protects against sunburn and the damaging of sweat glands. Others dispute this theory, claiming that a greater heat absorption by dark skin would be disadvantageous; that a light skin that reflects infra-red rays would be more advantageous from the point of heat absorption.

HAIR

Pigment in hair is also melanin, except for red hair in which a different pigment occurs. Red hair shows up among the Irish, Welsh, Scottish highlanders, Finns, and some Asians, but is generally rather uncommon. The most frequent hair color is brown; blonde hair is generally limited to people with light skins. The blonde hair of some Australian Aboriginal groups is unique since they have dark skins and eyes; children are born with blonde hair that darkens as they grow older.

Variations in hair can be in amount and distribution on human bodies as well as in texture and color. If we consider all groups of humans, the greatest concentration of hair is on the head, around the genitals, and in the armpits. Europeans tend to have more body hair than other groups. Asian populations, classified generally as Mongoloid, vary in amount of body hair, with the Japanese being an example of a group that has body hair comparable in amount to Europeans. Other Asians classed as Mongoloid have very little body hair. Africans, classed as Negroid, have little body hair; however people described as Oceanic Negroes often have a great deal of body hair.

The texture of hair depends on its diameter, cross-section, and linear form. In cross-section it may be from round to oval and of different degrees of flatness. In linear form it varies from straight to wavy to various degrees of curliness. In general, the flatter the cross-section of each individual hair the more spiral or curly it will be. Conversely, the more round the cross-section, the straighter the linear form.

Eyelashes can differ in length, density, and straightness or curl. Eyebrows are usually thick or thin according to general body hairiness. Australian Aborigines and Europeans, for example, may have heavy brows compared to Mongoloids.

EYES

Dark eyes are most common among all people. Eye color probably protects the inner eye from harmful sun rays; therefore, light-eyed people may be at a disadvantage in sunny regions. Although light eyes (blue, gray, and green) are most commonly correlated with lightly pigmented hair and skin, they also occur among dark people.

Opinions differ greatly about the possible adaptive aspects of dif-

Fig. 3–3. The blonde hair of some Australian Aboriginal groups is unique since they have dark skins and eyes. (David Moore for Black Star.)

ferent eye forms. The epicanthic fold, a fold of skin that covers part or all of the edge of the upper eyelid, is common among Mongoloids and Bushmen of Africa. Some biologists think it may be protection against the cold and snow glare for Mongoloids living in very cold regions and protection against sun glare for the Bushmen.[6]

BODY CONTOUR

Classification of human body types is difficult since the averages or the modes these types represent are likely to be emphasized, and people may overlook the wide range of human variations within populations. Averages and norms describe trends rather than the total picture. Downs and Bleibtreu contend that even population differences in height have been greatly exaggerated.[7] They underscore within-group variation by pointing out that "tall" pygmies of Africa or Indonesia may be taller than "short" Europeans or Japanese. Conversely, Crow Indians of North America or Nilots of Africa (groups noted for their tallness) may be shorter than "tall" Europeans or Japanese. Height has limited usefulness as a measure, for a measurement designating height conveys little information on components such as length of the head, neck, trunk, and leg or the proportional relations among these components. For example, the height of a Bushwoman in Africa would give no indication of the effect of steatopygia, the thick layer of fat on the thighs and buttocks, on her general body contour.[8]

One of the most ambitious attempts to examine human variation in body build is that of Sheldon, who classified American males and females of different races according to the degree to which they exhibit characteristics of three major body types: the endomorphic (rounded with prominent abdomen), mesomorphic (large boned and muscular), and ectomorphic (linear and fragile).[9] According to his explanation of his system, all individuals are considered to have some of each of the three types of characteristics even though they may be most closely identified as one type or another.

A basic problem in design and construction of body coverings is that the body is a three-dimensional form that must be fitted by flat materials such as fabrics, skins, leaves, and grasses. These materials must be suspended on, wrapped around, or fitted to the contours of the body. When fabrics are cut and sewn, design possibilities are multiplied in contrast to what is possible with suspended or wrap-around garments. The three-dimensional body is also adorned by three-dimensional materials such as precious stones and metals. In this case, hard or rigid objects must be accommodated to a potentially moving body.

Fig. 3–4. Sheldon's somatotypes from pp. 58–59 of Cohen's *Personality Assessment*. (From William H. Sheldon, *Atlas of Men*. New York: Harper & Row Publishers, Inc., 1954.)

Not only does each human being differ from all others in physical appearance, posture, and body movement, but the appearance of each individual also changes continuously, especially in the inevitable process of aging. A series of changes in height, weight, hair and skin color and texture, and general body contour take place with aging. Adjustments in clothing are often, therefore, responses to age changes. Until maturity, new clothes may be needed often in order to keep up with increases in body size. However, changes in body size

Fig. 3–5. The appearance of each individual changes continuously, especially in the inevitable process of aging.

and contour continue throughout life. Even height may change after maturity as skeletal changes take place. In addition, loss of subcutaneous fat deposits in the face occurs causing facial features to develop sharper or more angular lines, and body movement gradually becomes restricted as muscle fibers undergo change and joints no longer bend or rotate so easily. Baldness and graying of hair may accompany aging, but vary according to population and sex. Women, for example, rarely become bald, whereas men frequently do. As body contour and mobility change and as skin and hair alter, an individual may be prompted to choose different designs and colors in order to suit his aesthetic tastes or to adjust social customs in his society.

Differences in body proportions at different ages also affect design of clothing. The average young child has a head that is about one-fourth of his body length while the adult has a head nearer one-eighth of total body length. The legs increase in proportion to body length from about one-fourth to about half of body length. While male and female infants vary little in general body contour, by adolescence the pelvis of the female has widened in proportion to the rest of the body and her breasts have developed.[10]

summary

Human beings are basically much alike in physical appearance because they are part of one species, *Homo sapiens*. However, differences exist in the appearance of their bodies. These differences can be attributed to the influences of environment, heredity, and the aging process. Although heredity is fixed and the aging process inevitable, environmental influences can be modified by the application of technology. On one hand, the utilization of certain tools or techniques may encourage survival of people with specific body configurations. On the other hand, medical care and kind of nutrition may largely determine the body's development and appearance. Differences and changes in physical appearance affect the design and choice of items of dress, always in relation to aesthetic tastes and social customs.

4

BODY, DRESS AND ENVIRONMENT

The comfort and optimum functioning of the human body depend upon the physiology of the body as it interacts with physical environment and items of dress that serve as body covering. These items are usually referred to as clothing to emphasize their quality of covering, and hence their potential protective, or regulatory characteristics.

In this chapter we will be concerned with the flexibility of human beings in adapting to different environmental conditions that may affect comfort and functioning of the body. Some adaptations are made by the body itself, some are the result of natural selection that supports survival of certain genetic types, still others are possible because man can produce cultural devices such as clothing and shelter. Optimum adaptation will depend upon a combination of both body and cultural adaptation. In moist, tropical climates clothing may not be completely necessary for basic survival; however, it may be desirable for comfort and personal satisfaction. In extremely cold arctic areas, in temperate regions in winter, and in hot desert regions some kind of clothing, shelter, or thermal control is required for survival.

body and physiological
adaptation to environment

The body itself can make certain physiological adjustments to changes in the natural environment, particularly changes in temperature and oxygen content of the air. Many such changes take place daily as individuals move from indoors to outdoors, from rest to work, or as they are exposed to daily cyclic changes in temperature. If a period of time is required for an individual's body to make adjustments, he is described as going through a period of acclimatization. Although evidence is difficult to assess, scientists propose that genetic diversity is related to adaptation to habitat, that through processes of natural selection, operating through great lengths of time, certain body types have the best chances of survival and, therefore, become common to a particular environment.

Basic Body Adjustments

Because man is a mammal, he is warmblooded and possesses some internal body mechanisms for regulation of temperature. Some of these physiological means for maintaining body temperature are sweating, shivering, and the expansion or contraction of blood vessels so that varying amounts of heat are given off with changes in temperature and humidity. "Goose flesh" is a remnant of the animal reflex of raising hair; but only in a limited way can it increase the boundary area of relatively still, hence insulative, air around the body.[1]

The core temperature of the body of a human is about 98.6° F., and an individual can survive only within a limited body temperature range. Variations of as little as 2° to 3° from the core temperature interfere with bodily functions and threaten life. Temperature of the body shell or skin, however, is not so critical a factor—this tem-

Fig. 4–1. Sweating is, however, a major defense against over-heating.

perature rises and falls according to environmental conditions and apparently differences as great as 20° F. do not seriously disturb body functioning.[2]

To adapt to fluctuations in thermal environment the body does have means of maintaining thermal equilibrium, that is of lowering heat production or increasing heat loss. Heat may be lost through the skin by radiation, convection, and conduction and as sweat evaporates; it may also be lost as water evaporates in the lungs and as feces and urine are excreted. Sweating is, however, the body's major defense against overheating. In adjustments to the lowering of temperature, constriction of blood vessels in the skin occurs so that not as much heat is carried to the surface of the skin; if temperature rises, the same vessels dilate in order to facilitate delivery of heat to the surface of the skin where it is dissipated. If, however, outside temperature is greater than that of the body, heat loss through the skin by conduction, radiation, and convection is blocked; and sweat is the only means of cooling the skin. The sexes differ in certain characteristics related to thermal control.[3] Females have a thicker layer of subcutaneous fat than males and a greater number of sweat glands per unit area of the skin. Thus females have a wider comfort range than men: 80° F. to 91.4° F. for women, 82.4° F. to 87.8° F. for men. Theoretically they thus should be able to wear less protective body covering than men under similar environmental conditions without feeling discomfort.

Acclimatization

Acclimatization may be more important than inherited body build in adaptation to habitat. In *cold* climates increase in metabolic rate is a principle means of acclimatization. As a result of increased metabolic rate, the skin temperature of the acclimatized person becomes warmer and his susceptibility to frostbite is lessened.

Several body adjustments aid man's acclimatization to *heat*. Amount of sweating increases. The salt concentration in both sweat and urine decreases so that danger of a salt loss that will cause heat cramps is reduced. In addition, an increased volume of blood is circulated that maintains adequate blood flow and adequate blood pressure as blood vessels are dilated at the skin surface to give off heat.[4]

The people of Tibet and the high plateau region of the Andes are among the relatively few human populations that have lived and bred at altitudes over 10,000 feet.[5] Study of Andean Indians indicates that they have been able to survive because of ways in which their bodies acclimatize to compensate for low oxygen content of the air. Unless acclimatizing is completely accomplished asphyxia may occur and reproduction is impossible.

Monge describes the series of anatomical, physiological, and chemical reactions that take place in adaptation of the body as follows: "increase of the 'bellows function' of the lung; higher total blood and lung volumes and higher ratio of lung volume to total blood volume; and increased concentration of hemoglobin and total circulating hemoglobin."[6]

Genetic Adaptation

Although a high proportion of man's adaptations to environment are of his own contriving, some groups of people who have lived for many generations under extreme conditions of heat, cold, or dryness appear to have developed genetically transferable adaptations to environmental conditions. Through the centuries, those who have had the ability to adapt have survived to carry on the society; others have been eliminated by death or disease.

Many different opinions are held concerning the degree of genetic adaptation that has taken place among different peoples. Although exceptions may be cited, one generally supported theory is that relationships between body surface area and body volume may be a result of genetic adaptation. For example, people such as the Australian Aborigines and the Tuareg of the Sahara, who have lived for a number of generations in dry heat, have long-limbed lean

Fig. 4–2.   Body volume and skin surface area. With constant volume, the more linear individual has the larger area. (From C. Coon, S. Garn, and J. Birdsell, *Races: A Study of the Problems of Race Formation in Man,* 1950. Courtesy of Charles C. Thomas, Publisher.)

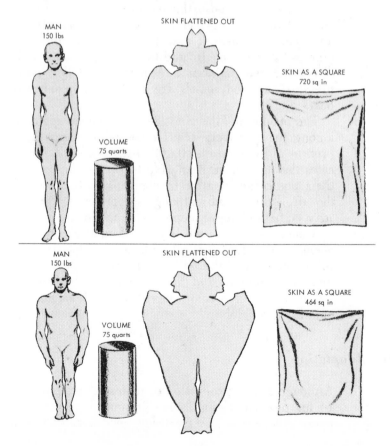

bodies with a proportionally large amount of body surface area to give off heat. In contrast, people like the Eskimos and others living around the Arctic circle have short extremities and rounded bodies that have a relatively small amount of skin surface in relation to their height and volume. Therefore, their bodies radiate proportionately less heat.

People who live in moist heat do not exhibit the same thin, lanky look as those in dry heat since they have high humidity to contend with. Thus the pygmies and forest people of Africa and the Indians of the humid Amazon-Orinoco basin, who must cope with difficulties of evaporation in a nearly saturated atmosphere, show no clear adaptation in body form.[7]

It is sometimes hypothesized that the facial structure of Mongoloid people is an adaptation that reduces injury due to cold. Small nose size and flattened brow ridges are considered adaptations that reduce exposure of the mucous membranes to the cold. Paddings of facial fat form a kind of insulative protection.

Some metabolic adaptation to cold seems to be inherited.[8] Alaskan Indians can sleep comfortably under conditions of moderate cold because they have an increased basal metabolic rate that is not affected by seasonal changes. Similar metabolic adaptation has been noted among Indians at the southernmost tip of South America. The Australian Aborigines also exhibit genetic adaptation to cold; however, their bodies make a different physiological adjustment, one that conserves body heat rather than generating heat through stepped-up metabolism. Apparently, temperature of the body core is maintained by intricacies of their circulatory systems that allow extremities, their arms and legs, to become cooled to low temperatures (as low as 54° to 59° F.) without discomfort. Under similar circumstances a Caucasian's body would act to maintain temperatures of extremities, resulting in a loss of body heat on the surfaces of arms and legs that would also cause internal body heat to be lost and discomfort to occur.

clothing and adaptation
to environment

Although the human being can make limited adjustments (both short term and long term) to environment through body adaptation, he is much more remarkable for his resourcefulness and versatility in

Fig. 4–3. Unlike lower animals, man can opt to be naked or to cover or shelter himself for survival in his climate. (From James F. Downs and Hermann K. Bleibtreu, *Human Variation: An Introduction to Physical Anthropology*, 1969. Glencoe Press of California.)

cultural adaptations. Unlike lower animals he has no protective hair, feathers, or down; however, he can opt to be naked, or to cover or shelter himself, at will. If he wants to survive in an adverse climate, for example, he may devise ways for providing an artificial environment that will insure his survival. Thus, he may conceive of how to build a house. Another solution is clothing, a compact and portable environment which, on an elementary level, is an "extension" of the temperature controlling mechanism of the body. Such

56

cultural adaptations can be accomplished relatively swiftly and simply and are effective where physiological adaptation alone could probably never insure survival, such as in arctic regions. In addition, they can be developed at many industrial levels, although the most elaborate contrivances are seen among highly industrialized people.

With his ability to devise cultural devices to facilitate his adaptation to environment, man can be freed from dependence on physiological or genetic adaptation, and can move into and shape new environments: he can create his own shields against physical environment. Clothing may be considered one of these shields; however, clothing does not isolate him completely from physical environment, for he still operates within it. Also clothing can create an environ-

Fig. 4–4. Clothing serves as a shield against physical environment. (Courtesy of Lenore Landry.)

ment for him. In other words clothing is an extension and modification of the body that may simultaneously be a portable environment and a means for intervening between individual and environment. Fourt and Hollies stress that:

It is important to realize that the clothing is not just a passive cover for the skin, but that it interacts with and modifies the heat regulating function of the skin and has effects which are modified by body movement. Some of this interaction is automatic, derived from the physical properties of the clothing materials and their spacing around the body; the larger scale interactions, however, arise from conscious choice of amount and kind of clothing, and mode of wearing, especially how the clothing is closed up or left open and loose.[9]

Thus they view clothing as a quasi-physiological system, which is an extension of the body and which interacts with the body.

As clothing serves as environment and interacts with the body it contributes to body comfort and health. In general this comfort and

Fig. 4–5.   Clothing may be considered a shield against the physical environment. The Hakka hats worn near Hong Kong shield the body from the sun. (Courtesy of Lenore Landry.)

Fig. 4–6. Clothing may be an extension and modification of the body simultaneously. (Courtesy of the Museum of Contemporary Crafts of the American Craftsman's Council from *Body Covering* exhibition, April 6–June 9, 1968, National Aeronautics Space Administration, Manned Spacecraft Center, Houston, Texas.)

health depend on maintenance of body temperature; provision of sufficient food, water, and oxygen; and protection against irritation and injury from outside agents or environmental forces. Clothing can aid in maintenance of body temperatures, can affect water needs, can be a protection against bodily injury, and in very specialized cases can provide a system supplying oxygen. Clothing requirements for various protective and maintenance purposes, however, depend upon other factors such as food intake, available shelter, and auxiliary heating or cooling systems. For protection and comfort, some balance among these factors must be maintained. If an insulated, enclosed shelter with a central heating system replaces the lean-to and open fire, obviously less clothing is required to achieve feelings of comfort. If air conditioning is introduced, warmer clothing may become necessary indoors. In cold climates, food intake can be stepped up to make more calories of heat available. If automobiles, trains, and planes have their own controlled environments within which people can be transferred from one controlled environment to another, adjustments to outside temperatures through clothing will become largely unnecessary.

Clothes as Extensions and Modification of the Body

Man is born with a functioning body as his basic equipment for securing comfort, satisfaction, and survival. His hands are good tools since he can gather food with them. His fists and teeth can be utilized as primitive weapons for defense. His opposable thumbs enhance his grasping ability and make him superior to the other primates as a tool user. His tool using can be supplemented through application of his highly developed brain in exploiting his environment or defending himself against environment. One of the things he can conceive of is how to equip himself with clothes in order to extend the effectiveness of his bodily efforts or to insure comfort and survival in adverse environments.

CLOTHES THAT EXTEND MOTOR SKILLS AND SPATIAL FORCE Two common kinds of clothes that extend a human being's use of his motor skills are foot and hand coverings. Man's basic means of transport are his own feet and the related motor skills that make locomotion possible. Footwear is one of the earliest cultural improvements in his self-propelled transportation, and some types of footwear have been especially useful in adapting to environment:

Fig. 4–7. Some footwear has been especially useful in adapting to the environment. (a) Apache painted leather boots, (b) Apache boots with typical southern band beading, (c) Eskimo waterproof sealskin boots ornamented by different colors of leather, and (d) waterproofed sealskin Eskimo boot. (Courtesy of Charles Miles.)

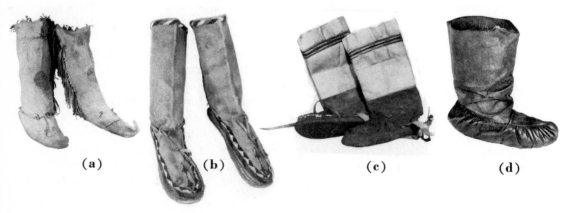

(a)   (b)   (c)   (d)

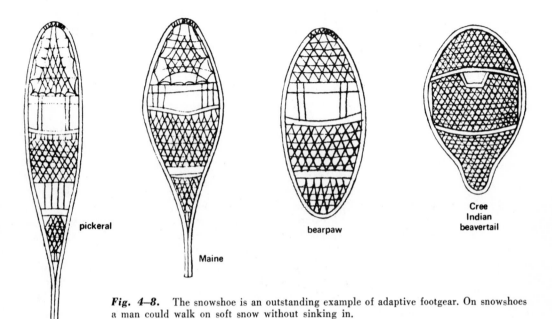

Fig. 4–8. The snowshoe is an outstanding example of adaptive footgear. On snowshoes a man could walk on soft snow without sinking in.

the furlined boot of the Eskimo and the sedge-lined shoes of the Lapps give protection against the cold; the moccasin of the American Indian provided protection against both cold and uneven terrain. Moccasins, however, were worn infrequently by Indians where it was warm and rained a great deal as in the southern part of North America. Heavy rainfall, canoeing, and fishing in the Northwest also discouraged use of the moccasin. Bock cites the snowshoe as one of the most outstanding examples of adaptive footgear.[10] Its historical significance was that it freed man from winter isolation that severely limited his communication and procuring of food: on snowshoes, a man could walk on soft snow without sinking in. The widespread use of the soft-soled moccasin in North America may have been related to the use of snowshoes, for the soft-soled moccasin made of a single piece of buckskin was easily used with snowshoes. Furthermore, although it was used beyond snowshoe areas, the moccasin's distribution corresponds closely with that of snowshoes in North America.[11] Snowshoes reached their highest development in North America—in Asia and Europe more attention was given to the development of skis that provided greater speed with less effort.[12]

The Lapps' reindeer skin shoes packed with sedge grass, are an outstanding example of footwear with excellent insulative quality. Milan reports the serious attention that Lapps give to their foot coverings as follows:

The Lapps neglect morning ablutions . . . but devote 20 minutes to dressing the feet. First, a dry pair of woolen socks are put on. A roll of sedge grass is then spread out on a reindeer skin and softened by wrinkling and twisting in the hands. If the grass was used the previous day and has passed the night stuffed in the shoe, it is thoroughly dried in the warmth of the fire. A rectangular pad of grass is wrapped around the clenched fist and inserted into the shoe. It must be of the same thickness on all sides. The foot is then placed in the shoe, and by wriggling and twisting and stuffing more grass down inside the shoe, a grass sock is gradually built up. The hem of the pants is then placed outside the shoe and the plaited lace, which is perhaps 3 feet long, is wound around the leg and secured. A Lapp will ski hard all day and by evening the grass sock is quite damp through perspiration. His feet remain warm even while resting for long periods in cold weather.[13]

Using gloves is one of the simplest ways to extend the body's mechanical capabilities. An individual's hands are excellent tools in themselves; but gloves give them protection against heat, cold, abrasion, and chemicals, and thus allow them to be used under very adverse environmental conditions. Firefighters, who face high temperature from flame, can extend their mobility with fireproof, reflective coverings, including gloves.

The football suit is an example of a kind of clothing which, as it protects the body, allows a player to exert and withstand force without bodily injury. Sometimes unique devices may be developed to extend body force. Navy researchers, for example, have explored the concept of a sort of body glove or exoskeleton that amplifies the muscular effort of man and increases his ability to do heavy work by utilizing the grasping power of the hands and the leverages of knees, elbows and other joints.[14] Artificial hands and other prosthetic devices that replace a missing body part are other unique extensions that enhance physical power and mechanical skills of the handicapped. False teeth may be placed in the same category.

CLOTHES THAT INTERVENE BETWEEN BODY AND CLIMATE

Although man can survive in tropical and subtropical areas without cultural aids, he usually can be made more comfortable with inventions such as clothing and shelter. In regions with constant severe cold, or periods of severe cold, he must have protective aids. Often the design of clothing has to be a compromise between temperature regulation and other kinds of environmental control, since clothes

Any exposure, at rest

6 hour exposure, at rest

Best possible mitten, good for
2-3 hours, at rest

Strenuous exercise,
no mitten needed

Fig. 4–9. Relative size of mitten needed for different exposure times at —20° F. (Adapted from Ralph F. Guttman, "The Arctic Soldier: Possible Research Solutions for His Protection," in Charles R. Kalb, ed., *Review of Research on Military Problems in Cold Regions*, A AL-TDR-64-28.)

Fig. 4–10. The football suit and helmet allow a player to increase the force he can exert and withstand. (Courtesy of Information Services, Michigan State University.)

may be serving several protective functions at the same time. Thus the enveloping robes of the nomads of the Sahara Desert not only protect against the sun's radiation but also against blowing sand. Other needs that may demand compromise are that of protection from dampness and from insects. Modesty requirements and desire for "attractiveness" in dress produce further compromise.

To simplify evaluations of clothing in relation to climate, Siple has proposed clothing zones of the world according to layers of clothing typically required. His classification is as follows:

1. The minimum clothing zone, or the humid tropical and jungle type.
2. The hot dry clothing zone, or desert type.
3. The one layer clothing zone, or subtropical or optimum comfort type.
4. The two layer clothing zone, or the temperate cool winter type.
5. The three layer clothing zone, or the temperate cold winter type.
6. The four layer maximum clothing zone, or subarctic winter type.
7. The activity balance zone, or the arctic winter type.[15]

A layer approach to dress, compatible with Siple's delineation, has been utilized by the United States military services in development of a fit-together "global uniform" concept. Thus the armed services have attempted to provide "basic units for the temperate zone to which items could be added for the colder, or subtracted for the warmer, zones so that tropical gear could be close to U.S. summer equipment, and polar gear added to the U.S. winter uniform." [16] In the section that follows are examples of kinds of clothing adaptations in areas of the world located in different climatic zones.

In the *minimum clothing zone* of the tropics clothing is not designed for thermal protection. However, protection from the sun for skin and eyes, and protection from pathogenic organisms, thorns, and insects, is likely to be related to the use of clothing. Otherwise, body covering is a matter of fashion and custom. Some kind of lightweight, loose garment of absorbent material, shading head gear that provides air space between hat and head, and perhaps sandals to protect the soles of the feet are probably adequate for protective purposes in the tropics.

In *hot dry clothing zones* adaptations are made to strong radiation from the sun and sharp differences in day and night temperatures. Desert nomads of North Africa have long worn long loose tunics of cotton or wool and fairly thick wool or mohair robes that cover arms

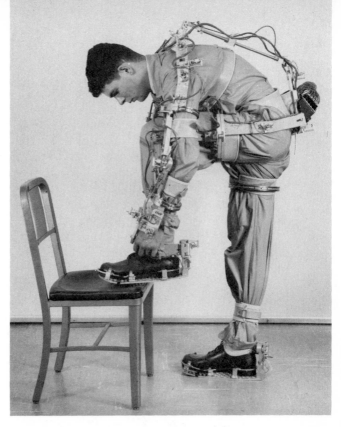

Fig. 4–11. This experimental exoskeleton is an example of man's attempt to expand his body capabilities. (Courtesy of Cornell Aeronautical Laboratory, Inc.)

and legs. These tent-like garments allow evaporation of sweat, which is facilitated by the air currents created by walking. Solar heat can be absorbed on the surface of the garments at a distance from the body.

The Bushmen of the Kalahari Desert of South Africa have not utilized enclosing body coverings in adapting to desert conditions. They appear to be partially acclimated to the daytime heat; however, scientists have not been able to determine if they have any particular adaptation to the nighttime cold. What is more certain is that the Bushmen have developed certain unique cultural aids to help them survive and be comfortable. At night the Bushman curls up in a skin cloak which he tucks in around his head and trunk, then places his feet, his face, or back to the fire, and uses his hut as a windbreak. "He coats his skin with plant juices and fats and, when obtainable, animal fat or blood, and accumulates a fine layer of Kalahari sand on the surface." [17] This "protective mail" assists his adjustment to hot conditions by protecting him from undue absorption of solar radiation and from the desiccating effects of hot, dry winds. During the winter, an ointment made from the tsama melons is smeared over the body and vigorously rubbed into the skin. "In the very dry atmosphere of the Kalahari in winter time this treatment has about the same beneficial effect as the application of cold cream to the exposed skin surfaces of the European." [18]

Siple hypothesizes that the *one layer or subtropical zone* presents ideal conditions for fashion to develop since climate places no great demand or restriction on dress. Thermal protection is needed for only the trunk region of the body and hands and feet require no special cover. Thus in North Central Europe in the summertime, Florida in the winter, Canada in the summer, and most of the United States in the spring and fall a single layer of clothing is sufficient to provide comfort, and a wide range of materials can be used. Fashion determines the details. [19]

The *two layer clothing zone* frequently is humid and has occasional wet snowfalls. Southern Alaska, British Columbia, the Northwest Coast of the United States, and the West Coast of Ireland are examples of areas that have this type of temperate, cool climate with considerable rain. Clothing must keep off rain as well as insulate against heat loss. Indians of the coastal areas of Northwest United States and Western Canada had protective wear especially suitable for a temperate rainy climate and their activities. Their basketry hats, worn for rain and sun, were waterproof but also served to protect them from the glare of sunlit water while canoeing or fishing. Flared rain capes of shredded red-cedar bark—made to hang just below the elbow—repelled water at the same time that they allowed arm movement for paddling canoes or engaging in other activities. Neckbands of fur prevented the harsh bark fiber from irritating the skin around the neck. [20]

In the winter much of Europe, Asia, and Africa fall into the *three and four layer cold-temperate and subarctic zones,* as do Arctic and Antarctic regions in the summer. Except for some very high altitude regions the zone is virtually absent in South America, Africa, Australia, and New Zealand.

Effective clothing for protection against cold in a subarctic area must have a high insulative value when a person is inactive, but a design that will allow dissipation of body heat when he is active. Otherwise the body will become heated, sweating will occur, and an accumulation of unevaporated sweat will cause chilling. Siple elaborates on problems involved in learning to use one's clothing in extreme cold as follows:

Individuals who are exposed to low temperatures at a degree of activity insufficient to produce comfortable thermo-balance must learn a multitude of technics which may increase the potential value of their protective clothing many times. In the first place, the body must become acclimatized so that it conserves heat to the maximum extent. Next, it is necessary that the garments are so fitted that there is maximum dead air space included between the clothing layers. Finally, there is the art of ventilating to avoid sweating, and in tightening closures to control too rapid loss of body heat. Each individual has to learn through experience how to perform these tasks.

No amount of reading will ever make a sourdough out of a tenderfoot upon first exposure to cold. The greenhorn in regions of extreme cold is apt to suffer unmercifully, whereas the experienced person has not only learned to tolerate the cold but is efficiently making adjustments after he has started to sweat. The sourdough never reaches the point of sweating if he can avoid it. The tenderfoot who has opened his clothing or taken off a garment rarely buttons up again until he is beginning to shiver. He seems to want to impress himself or others with the appearance of being "tough enough to take it." The sourdough puts his clothing on and closes up before he begins to get chilled, and he stays warmer much longer.[21]

The general solution for what to wear in a very cold climate is, therefore, to find a light-weight material that will not load the wearer down, a way of trapping insulative dead air spaces between loose-fitting layers of clothing, and a design that can be opened up easily for releasing warm, moist air that may accumulate around the body during activity.[22]

The Eskimo solution to cold has been to wear loosely fitting tailored garments of fur, most commonly caribou and seal, sometimes polar bear, fox, and bird skins.[23] A belt, worn over shirt and undershirt, which hang outside trousers, may be used to control temperature. By loosening this belt, throwing back the parka hood, and taking off mittens or a layer of garments an Eskimo can cool off. When at rest he draws his arms out of sleeves and puts them close to his body to keep them warm. Sweat control is very important because wet garments lose their insulative value. Therefore, garments are often taken off inside and must be carefully dried if they become wet.

In the *activity balance zone* no increase beyond four layers of garments is effective for protection; garments become too bulky for wear. Other types of protective measures need be taken. Activity will be required for survival outdoors. Another possible solution is an auxiliary heating system, especially for hands and feet, which are very difficult to keep warm in extreme cold. Otherwise, shelter will be required.

Fig. 4–12. Diving suits are one of the oldest types of outfits that have approached providing a total environment. (Courtesy of Aqua-Lung, Division of U.S. Divers Co.)

Dress as Total Environment

Diving suits are one of the oldest types of outfits that have approached providing a total environment for the man who is facing a hazardous environment, nonsupportive of human life. More recently some ventilated protective suits have been produced for workers needing protection against radiation, noxious gases, and dangerous chemicals. The space suit, however, is the most complicated costume that man has yet invented as a total environment. Suits for various space trips have varied; however, they all have provided ways to sustain body functions while allowing body mobility.[24] They have included systems for removing metabolic heat, carbon dioxide, water vapor, urine, and fecal matter and for providing oxygen and external (gaseous) pressure; helmets are designed to allow vision but keep out harmful radiation; the layers of the suit, including flameproof woven fabrics and aluminized plastic films, protect from meteoroids as well as the extreme heat and cold of space; an integral part of suits have been bioinstrumentation systems that allow space control stations to keep constant check on

Fig. 4–13. The space suit is the most complicated costume that man has yet invented as a total environment. (Courtesy of NASA.)

Fig. 4–14. Features of protective space suits may effect designs for streetwear. This poncho, which is made of the same aluminized plastic film used in space suits, is claimed to be capable of radiating 80 percent of body heat back to the wearer. (Courtesy of the *New York Times.*)

blood pressure, heart action, body temperature, and respiration rate; microphones and headsets for interspace communication are also part of regular equipment. Features of protective space suits may affect street wear. Offered for sale in 1970 was a poncho made from the same aluminized plastic film used in space suits.

summary

Man's adaptation to various natural environments depends to some extent upon short-term adaptations to environment that his body can make and on genetic types of adaptation evolving through many generations. To a much larger extent his adaptation depends upon the cultural aids he can devise to supplement his basic biological equipment and to intervene between his body and environment. Clothing is one of the most universally used types of cultural aids.

Dress can affect motor skills of individuals as well as protect them. The need for clothing as a protection against climate depends upon seasonal changes as well as geographical area. In extreme cold, clothing can be effective as insulative protection only so long as it does not seriously hinder body movement. For example, when clothing required for protection becomes so bulky as to prevent mobility, other protective devices must be introduced. The space suit is an example of a type of clothing that is a portable life support control system, providing for all needs except food and water.

III

DRESS as ART

5

THE PURSUIT OF BEAUTY

finding beauty in dress

The cliche that "beauty is in the eye of the beholder" is at least a part truth as far as dress and appearance are concerned. Most evaluations of the aesthetic merit of dress and dress in relation to the body stem from *visual* reactions to color, the play of light and shadow, the relation of lines and form. However, other organs of perception also register aesthetic responses. Perhaps the skin receives some of our most primitive aesthetic sensations because our first contacts with the world are largely through the sense of touch. A baby's world extends, in general, only as far as he touches and feels—he responds to the feeling of his clothes or swaddlings, learns to react with pleasure to the touch of his mother, notices feelings of being wet or dry, and learns to love the texture of a favorite toy.

Our ears allow us to find pleasure in recognizable forms of sound and combinations of sound, identifiable most commonly as music, poetry, and prose. The aesthetic worth of written words lies in their potential tonal qualities, rhythms, and cadence, as well as uniqueness of expression. Performing artists—musicians, poets, readers— translate the printed symbol into sound. Their dress is designed to support their presentations. Occasionally everyday dress produces sound, as in the case of a rustling petticoat or jangling bracelets. More often sound-producing devices are a part of festive, ceremonial, or theatrical dress.

Although odors are rarely thought of as an essential part of costume, scents (both real as in flowers or manufactured as in perfumes), soaps, and lotions, are common accessories of dress. In addition, the characteristic odors of common materials used in making clothing may have some aesthetic appeal. Leather, for example, gives off distinct odors that are developed during processing of skins. Whether these odors are pleasing simply because of themselves, or the associations they provoke due to their familiarity, is debatable. Perhaps both factors are influential, as they may be in the case of the American housewife who finds that clothes dried in

Fig. 5–1. Some American housewives find that clothes dried in the open air have a desirable fragrance.

the open air have a more desirable fragrance for her than those dried in a mechanical dryer. In all these cases, scent is the stimulus that evokes pleasurable responses that in turn presumably add to aesthetic satisfactions with the body and its dress. The antiquity of the inspiration to cultivate olfactory pleasure is suggested by recent studies of pollen and flower fragments found in a Neanderthal burial site in Iraq. These finds indicate that an appropriate tribute to the dead may have been to lay them to rest in a fragrant bed of flowers.[1]

Therefore, personal beauty is associated with some kind of pleasurable feeling or emotion that arises with stimulation of man's sensory organs, as well as with human evaluations of what the senses record, rather than with provable facts concerning quality of beauty. Santayana stresses these qualities in all beauty as he says:

Beauty is a value . . . it is an emotion, an affection of our volitional and appreciative nature. An object cannot be beautiful if it can give pleasure to nobody: a beauty to which all men were forever indifferent is a contradiction in terms.

In the second place, this value is positive, it is the sense of the presence of something good, or (in the case of ugliness) of its absence. It is never the perception of a positive evil, it is never a negative value.[2]

His definition distinguishes beauty from another kind of human value which is commonly applied to dress, that is, the moral value. Moral values, unlike aesthetic values, are on the whole negative; they are perceptions of the wrong or evil. They are being exercised, for example, when we are admonished by precept, or by the internalized voice of conscience, not to strike another human being or to judge his physical beauty. In Santayana's terms, the pursuit of beauty strives for the attainment of pleasure, whereas the main concern of morals is prevention of suffering.

The existence of human beings who can respond to stimuli in a sensory way, and in a psychologically and culturally evaluative way, is prerequisite to development of an idea of what beauty is; however, beauty can only be identified after some recognizable form persists for some length of time. Establishment of a recognizable form depends on the mastery of a technical skill and societal recognition of the value of the form, which occurs through time. Martindale explains the establishing of forms that are judged as beautiful in this way:

If there is a general lesson to be learned from the study of primitive art, it seems to be that the appearance of art is promoted by the stability of a com-

*munity form within which a progressive mastery of basic techniques is pos-
sible. Whenever sufficient mastery of basic techniques is possible to permit
the occurrence of standard forms, these tend to be subject to purely formal
criteria of beauty. Sometimes long periods of time seem to be necessary to
accomplish this reality. However, there seems hardly to be an activity, so
long as it is capable of producing standard forms, which may not be seized
upon for aesthetic manipulation and enjoyment.*[3]

Ideas about personal beauty, therefore, can evolve as a society
seizes upon particular forms of body and dress from which they are
able to derive pleasurable emotions and as it develops techniques
that promote persistence in form.

the universal pursuit
of personal beauty

Adornment of the body, including dressing of hair and using of
cosmetics, is indulged in by all cultural groups.[4] The casual observer may be first impressed by a seemingly endless world variety in
body decoration, but his more overwhelming discovery is that all
peoples use costume to beautify themselves, though for a variety
of reasons. The adornment may be only a little paint, a necklace,
or a waist-string, but it *is* decoration that, deliberately or inadvert-
ently, reveals an individual's unique talents, his outlooks, and his
sentiments. The enthusiasm for body ornament is a personal as well
as a social matter, for not all are equally disposed to use dress as a
means for self-beautification. Although man is by nature social and
lives in groups for survival, he also dwells in a private, individual
existence and screens group norms when deciding upon personal
action. He, therefore, may faithfully follow standards for beauty
in his own society or modify them for idiosyncratic reasons.

No matter how an individual interprets beauty, some element of
the aesthetic exists in his dress as long as he covers or grooms his
body in the slightest way. Two of the most unclad peoples of the
world, and certainly the best-known, have been the Indians of Tierra
del Fuego at the southernmost tip of South America and the aboriginal people of central Australia. Both groups traditionally with-
stood great extremes of temperature with little body covering or
shelter.

The Fuegians were picturesquely described by Charles Darwin in
his journal that recorded observations made during the famous sur-

(a)

Fig. 5–2. Adornment of the body is an activity indulged in by all cultural groups, as shown by (a) Korean dress, (b) West African wrapper, and (c) Western ball gown. (Courtesy of (a) *State Journal* photo by Ginger Sharp, (b) Joanne B. Eicher, and (c) *Vogue*, copyright 1968 by The Condé Nast Publications Inc.)

(b)

(c)

veying expedition of the ship Beagle between 1831-36. These people either wore no coverings or tossed scant fur mantles of guanaco, otter, or sealskin about their shoulders in a way scarcely likely to keep them warm. As Darwin's description of one of their leaders reveals, however, they were not without body decoration. The old man he described

> *. . . had a fillet of white feathers tied round his head, which partly confined his black, coarse, and entangled hair. His face was crossed by two broad transverse bars; one, painted bright red, reached from ear to ear and included the upper lip; the other white like chalk extended above and parallel to the first so that even his eyelids were thus coloured.*[5]

The nomadic Aborigines of central Australia also survived under adverse environmental conditions with no coverings and only simple lean-tos of brush to protect them. Desert conditions which allowed temperatures to go below freezing did not induce them to invent any kind of protective clothing; however, like the Fuegians they decorated their bodies—with paint, scars, or emu down glued on with blood.[6]

Even coverings that are intended only to meet climatic demands for protection or social requirements for modesty have some element of the decorative and elicit some aesthetic response. Mahatma Gand-

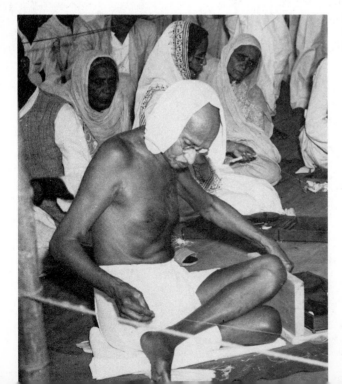

Fig. 5–3. Mahatma Gandhi's dress exemplified minimized personal display but had decorative elements. (Courtesy of Wide World Photos.)

hi's dress exemplified minimal personal display; yet it had decorative elements. His white loin cloth, which contrasted with his olive skin, stimulated an aesthetic reaction to color. His spectacles helped him see, but they also became part of his facial configuration and hence subject to visual responses by those who viewed him. Therefore, as clothing covers, it also decorates, in the sense that it modifies possible visual responses to the combinations of line, shape, texture, and color that can be made toward the covered as versus the uncovered body.

Although interest in personal beauty is universal, the way in which this interest is interwoven into the lives of people within different cultural conditions may be quite dissimilar. On the one hand, in a society with a simple technology expression of personal beauty may be intertwined closely with nearly all aspects of the culture: with ritual, religion, work, family life, systems of social control. On the other hand, in a technologically complex society expressions of personal beauty may be interrelated with some but not all aspects of culture.

unity and variety in form of dress

Scholars have agreed that the pursuit of beauty is universal and have been intrigued with how to analyze the variety of forms of body decoration and covering that have been used in this pursuit. In the early 1930s Goldenweiser proposed that "a limitation of possibilities checks variety" [7] in cultural features—that, given similar goals or similar problems to solve, societies will arrive at similar types of solutions. Such convergence appears in the design of costume, and is seen in both covering and ornament. Dressing a three-dimensional form like the body places certain limits on the kinds of materials used and the kinds of techniques that can be used to apply or assemble them. Trial and error sorts out those materials and techniques that are most effective in creating desired effects. No design can be developed and utilized that completely impedes body functioning. In addition, materials used must fulfill certain requirements if they are to be fitted to, or adjusted to, body structure in some way: fabric coverings must be pliable; metal for jewelry must be malleable in some way; body paints must adhere to the skin.

Unity in the variety of the forms of dress can be found if they are classified as predominantly *reconstructing, enclosing,* or *attached.*

Reconstructing types of dress include temporary or permanent changes in body conformation, texture, color, or odor that are thought to have some beautifying effect. Plastic surgery may reform a nose, chin line, or breast into a shape thought more beautiful than the original. Knocking out of teeth or cutting of hair are enhancements through removal of body parts (similar practices may be noted in the clipped ears or tails of show dogs). Texture changes done in the name of beauty include scarring of skin and waving and straightening of hair, for which combs, brushes, curlers, and hair pins are used. Pressure bindings may be used to change many aspects of body form—cranial shape, foot size and shape, waist size and placement have sometimes been modified. Paints,

Fig. 5–4. Reconstructed ear of a man from Kenya. (Courtesy of Richard W. Reierson.)

Fig. 5–5. Reshaping of hair as exemplified by this Nigerian woman is an often-used type of body reconstruction. (Courtesy of Carl K. Eicher.)

Fig. 5–6. This Hausa woman from northern Nigeria shows how texture changes are used to create beauty by reconstructing the skin by scarring. (Courtesy of the Federal Ministry of Information, Lagos, Nigeria.)

Fig. 5–7. Pressure bindings may be used to change many aspects of body form, as in the case of this Koskimo Kwakiutl woman of Vancouver Island whose long tapering head was achieved by binding between two padded boards as an infant—a mark of beauty among the Northwest Coast Indians. (Courtesy of Information Canada Phototheque.)

Fig. 5–8. Body paint as applied by an American. (Courtesy of the Maybelline Co.)

chalks, oils, lotions, scents, and powders are common "beautifying materials" used alone or in some combination to create changes in the color, texture, or odor of skin and hair. Permanent color changes can be made in hair by dyeing and bleaching, in skin by tattooing.

Enclosing forms may be *suspended, wraparound, fitted,* or some combination thereof. Circular forms like necklaces, pendants, and ponchos with openings for the head are *suspended* forms that may be readily conceived of by a people, since they slip on the body fairly easily and will stay in place as they hang from neck and shoulders.

Wraparound items include waist strings, sashes, some jewelry, as well as more encompassing coverings like the traditional sari of India and Pakistan. In all these items a form of greater length

Fig. 5–9. Body paint as applied by the Pondo of South Africa. (Courtesy of Percy Wannerton, Rainbow Transparancies, Capetown, South Africa.)

Fig. 5–10. Permanent color changes can be made in the skin by tattooing. In (a) a Milwaukee, Wisconsin girl has a rose tattooed on her arm; in (b) a Nigerian girl has her face tattooed. (Courtesy of (a) the *Milwaukee Journal*, and (b) the Federal Ministry of Education, Lagos, Nigeria.)

(a)

(b)

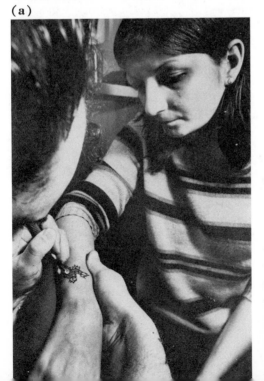

Fig. 5–11. These suspended, attached, and fitted types of body ornaments have long been used by Masai women in achieving personal beauty. (Courtesy of Richard W. Reierson.)

Fig. 5–12. A necklace is a suspended form of dress. (Courtesy of *Vogue*, copyright 1968 by The Condé Nast Publications Inc.)

Fig. 5–13. A poncho is a suspended form of dress. (Courtesy of *Vogue*, copyright 1970 by The Condé Nast Publications Inc.)

than width is predominant, although in the larger coverings, circles, semicircles, triangles, trapezoids, and miscellaneous other shapes as well as rectangles are used. To facilitate wrapping, however, all shapes are manipulated by folding, crushing, or twisting so that the form approaches the rectangular. A study of the changing appearance of the Roman toga reveals that different sizes and shapes of cloth were used as the garment evolved, but a greater length than width was a necessary basis for its drapery.

Fig. 5–14. Nigerian women's wrappers and head ties are wraparound forms of dress. (Courtesy of the Federal Ministry of Information, Lagos, Nigeria.)

Fig. 5–15. Masai warriors wear wraparound garments. (Courtesy of Richard W. Reierson.)

Fig. 5–16. The bracelets and wrist rings are fitted to the body of the Ndebele woman while the large neck ring appears to be suspended. (Courtesy of Percy Wannerton, Rainbow Transparencies, Capetown, South Africa.)

Fitted forms include rings, bracelets, rigid waist bands, and fillets that fit body crevices or protuberances. Also fitted are shoes, hats, trousers, jackets, and tunics that are either cut and sewed or molded to conform closely to body contour.

Some forms of enclosing dress cannot be easily classified in one of the foregoing three categories. As an example, the kimono is both wraparound and somewhat fitted; some capes are fitted, suspended, and wraparound. A form of enclosing dress that has elements classifiable in more than one category may be called a *combined form*.

Attached ornament is often closely allied with body reconstruction. Pierced ears and septums are examples of reconstructions that

Fig. 5–17. The woman's pants suit is an example of a fitted form of dress. (Courtesy of Celanese®.)

Fig. 5–18. The bullfighter's suit is an example of a fitted form of dress. (Courtesy of *Vogue*, copyright 1971 by The Condé Nast Publications Inc.)

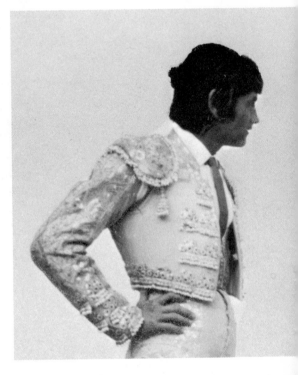

Fig. 5–19. The Peruvian face mask is an unusual example of a fitted form of dress. (Courtesy of the Museum of Contemporary Crafts of the American Craftsmen's Council, from *Face Covering* exhibition, September 30, 1970–January 3, 1971, Girard Foundation.)

Fig. 5–20. A form of enclosing dress that has elements classifiable in more than one category may be called a combined form. (Courtesy of Japanese National Tourist Organization.)

Fig. 5–21. The nosering and earrings of this Nigerian woman are attached forms of dress. (Courtesy of the Federal Ministry of Information, Lagos, Nigeria.)

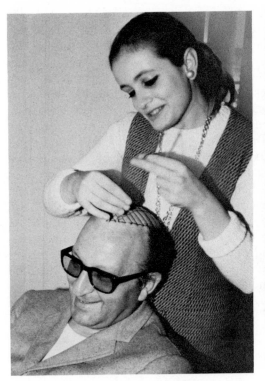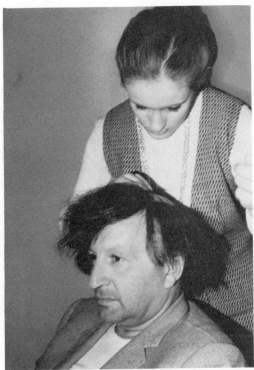

Fig. 5–22. A proposed sewn-on hairpiece touted in the popular press of 1969 is a form of attached dress. (Courtesy of Lloyd Shearer, from *Parade*, October 19, 1969.)

some attached ornaments require. Piercing of the scalp for a proposed sewn-on hairpiece touted in the popular press of 1969 is another example.[8] Clip and screw type earrings represent technical solutions for attached ear ornaments that depend on pressure for attachment rather than change of body form. Pins and brooches are attachments fastened to removable coverings rather than to the body itself.

Unity in form of dress, therefore, is not found in identical materials or in execution of designs. Instead similarities in classification, not content or specific details, must be determined in order to perceive unity. Types of covering or adornment for the body—that is, reconstructing, enclosing, or attached—exemplify universal solutions for dressing the body.

Examples of variety in suspended, enclosing forms of dress include the Mexican version of the poncho, the *quechquemitl;* the

Ecuadorian poncho; necklaces from many parts of the world; the priest's chasuble. In the category of wraparound forms we can find the Ethiopian *shamma,* the Indian sari, the Yoruba wrapper, the Scottish kilt, and turbans. Among fitted forms are bracelets and rings of many types, sweaters, trousers, shoes, bowlers, and top hats. Binding to form the Chinese lotus foot, scarification, and corseting are examples of reconstructing types of dress that alter body conformation or texture. Reconstruction of body color is exemplified by the body painting of the Tchrikin of Brazil and by the tattooing of the early Maori of New Zealand. Shaving lotions, fingernail polish, lipstick, rouge, and eye shadow are contemporary Western ways of changing (reconstructing) body color or odor. Variations among attached forms can be seen in many types of earrings; nose, lip, and chin ornaments; and pins, combs, and barrettes.

These diverse solutions allow people to achieve order in and pleasure from coverings and adornment of the body, and relationship between them and parts of the body. From these orderly relationships pleasure is derived and assessment of beauty results.

summary

All people in some way endeavor to beautify themselves. In addition, each person reacts to the aesthetic stimuli that dress provides. Although his major aesthetic reactions are to what he sees, he may also be sensitive to sounds, such as those created by jangling bracelets, to the textures of various items of dress, and to the odors of perfumes and lotion. Personal beauty in dress is difficult to define. However, it may be regarded as identifiable relationships between body and dress, recognized by a culture group, and capable of giving emotional satisfaction and pleasure to both wearer and observer.

Although many specific variations can be noted in the dress that people wear, an underlying unity can be determined if the forms of dress are classified as predominantly reconstructing, enclosing, or attached.

6

IDEALS FOR PERSONAL BEAUTY

In all societies some forms of appearance are singled out as having desirable aesthetic qualities, while others are rejected. As consensus on what is considered most beautiful is approached, cultural ideals for personal beauty evolve. These ideals, based on evaluations of the characteristics of both body and dress, exist as goals and may be achieved by only a few people.

Cultural standards for beauty are distinguished from ideals, for a standard must be real and achievable by many people. When measurements can be made, reality of a standard is verified. For example, if a standard length for a woman's dress at a particular time is ten inches from the floor, congruity with the standard can be determined. On the other hand, no such exact measure can be used to determine ideal facial form.

(a)

(b)

(c)

Fig. 6–1. No exact measure can be used to determine ideal facial form; variations always exist. (Courtesy of (a) *Vogue,* copyright 1968 by The Condé Nast Publications Inc., (b) Lenore Landry, and (c) Richard W. Reierson.)

An individual's likes and dislikes in regard to beauty are not haphazard. Instead, they are predictable preferences dependent upon the social context within which the individual learns to view his world. He learns cultural ideals and standards whereby he can make judgments. Identification of ideals and standards for beauty is possible within specific social contexts, seldom worldwide; therefore, beauty must be understood as a social variable. Personal beauty does not exist in the absolute sense; it is always viewed in relation to a specific cultural situation.

Ideals are ordinarily assumed to be common knowledge although occasionally they are stated explicitly. In addition, ideals may be presented either positively as "perfect," or negatively as problems. They may also be expressed as ideals for beautiful body form, beautiful dress, or beautiful relationships between body and dress.

ideals in body form

Variations in ideals for body types (including facial forms) can be readily ascertained by looking at visual presentations of human figures, either male or female, in any society. If Greek and Gothic female nudes from art work, twentieth century fashion figures, and the playgirl of the month are compared, different body proportions can be noted. Similar variations can be noted by comparing the breast, waist, and hip measurements of Venus de Milo, Brigitte Bardot, and Twiggy. (Venus de Milo, 37-26-38; Brigitte Bardot, 36-22-36; Twiggy, 30½-24-33).[1] The Greek nude female figure fits a classical standard that requires the same unit distance between breasts, from breasts to navel, and from navel to division of the legs. In Gothic figures the distance from breasts to navel is almost twice as great as between breasts.[2] Recently American fashion figures have been tall and slender, therefore rather Gothic in effect. The playgirl is a more rounded type.

The Greeks' great regard for physical perfection, which they linked with "excellence of soul or spirit," was reflected in their emphasis upon gymnastics as well as in their art.[3] That as long ago as the time of the Greeks, the obese body did not measure up to standards for bodily excellence is suggested by a vase figure of a young man who, it appears, is being reproached by one of his more lithe companions.

Fig. 6–2. Rejection of the plump figure among the Greeks is suggested by a scene painted on a Greek vase. (Attic vase, early 5th century B.C., Palaestra scene. Courtesy of the British Museum, London, England.)

Ideals for body form demonstrate the power of cultural ideals within a society. Considerable consensus exists on what is the most beautiful in body build, and almost everyone understands what the standards are even when they are not explicitly stated. Thus Jacqueline Kennedy Onassis, at the same time she is being judged by the popular press to be beautiful, can be chided in having "an outsized head" and "a size 10 shoe." [4]

body and dress

Although no costume can be completely independent of the human form, a continuum exists between that most nearly merging with body form and that which greatly diverges from body form. Many costumes seem to stand more by themselves as items of independent artistic merit than as complements to body form: the women's bustle costume of the 1870s and 1880s, the ornate and heavily padded sixteenth century costume of Henry VIII, the dragon robe of the Chinese emperor; and the twentieth century Nigerian *agbada*. By contrast, a closely fitting flesh-colored body stocking, diverging from body form only in texture, closely merges with body form. A thin application of paint creates divergence in color, perhaps in texture, but not in shape; the closer the color of the paint is to body color, the more it merges with body, the less it diverges.

One example of shifting standards in the history of Western dress can be seen in the fluctuation in form of dress that merges with,

Fig. 6–3. The woman's bustle costume stands more by itself than as a complement to body form.

Fig. 6–4. Henry VIII's costume epitomizes ornate dress that minimizes visual impact of body form. (From Cecil W. and Phyllis Cunnington, *Handbook of English Costume in the 16th Century*, rev. ed. 1962. Reprinted by permission of the Hillary House Publishers, and Faber and Faber, Ltd.)

versus that which diverges from body form. One of the sharpest
shifts from costume that diverged from body form came at the end
of the eighteenth century when hoops, pompadoured wigs, and stiff,
heavily brocaded fabrics were abandoned for more close fitting,
less colorful clothing. Men wore jackets and snug tubular trousers
of plain colors, and women were said to have oiled their skins so
that their narrow white muslin dresses would cling to their bodies.[5]
By the middle of the nineteenth century men's body contours were
lost in loose-fitting suits and females concealed the lower parts of
their bodies under voluminous hoop skirts.

Ideals which pertain to the relation between body and dress are
often subtle. Subordination of dress to body has been a persistent
Western ideal for men's dress for more than a hundred years. And,
as commentary on women's dress makes plain, an expression of a
similar ideal for women's dress has occurred from time to time.
As long ago as 1879 Mrs. Haweis, an English woman, said that
dress "shall not contradict the natural lines of the body" and
"shall obey the proportions of the body." [6] In the 1960s Horn
stated that "beauty of silhouette is achieved when the costume does
not contradict or obscure the pleasing relationships of the form be-
neath it," and Latzke and Hostetter declared: "A good dress design
is always related to body structure . . . it generally follows body
contours, but does not exaggerate these contours in any way." [7]
Fluctuation over time in the ideal relationships of body and dress
make it obvious that whether dress is subordinate to the body or
body to dress is a matter of custom and fashion and not a timeless
generalization.

Fig. 6–5. Knit fabrics which stretch themselves around the body form are subordinate to the body.
(Courtesy of *Vogue,* copyright 1970 by The Condé Nast Publications Inc.)

Fig. 6–7. The body form is subordinate to this voluminous tent dress. (Courtesy of *Vogue*, copyright 1971 by The Condé Nast Publications Inc.)

Fig. 6–6. Clothing subordinate to body is exemplified by these black nightgowns. (Courtesy of Celanese®.)

Fig. 6–8. The habit of these nuns subordinates body to dress. (Courtesy of Richard Sharpe.)

examples of ideals
within different societies

Historical contrasts in Western ideals for beauty of body form have been described by Antubam.[8] Among the ancient Egyptians the female ideal was typified by Nefertiti (c. 1370 B.C.) who had a straight nose, long neck, oval head, and deeply-set, large eyes. The Mesopotamian male ideal was that of a conqueror whose strength and power were reflected in large and often over-emphasized muscles. The Greek ideals for male and female were epitomized by Apollo and Venus de Milo, both sturdy and well-formulated figures. The Italian Renaissance ideal was exemplified by Botticelli's slender-bodied Venus while the Dutch Renaissance ideal was shown in the voluptuously ample proportions of Ruben's Venus.

Ghana

Antubam also provides detail on Ghanaian ideals for female beauty, which vary sharply from Western ideals presented above. Among Ghanaians many parts of the body are described as egg-shaped ovals. For example, the shape of the head from the top of

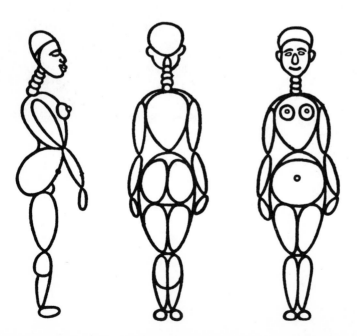

Fig. 6–9. Ghanaian ideals of beauty are prescribed by specific patterns of ovals. (Courtesy of Kofi Antubam, *Ghana's Heritage of Culture*, 1963, Koehler and Amelang.)

the head to the end of the chin is expected to look like an egg with the wider portion uppermost. "Looked at from the side, the head must set on the neck at an angle of about thirty-five degrees with the top part falling back." The traditional Ghanaian *Akuaba* fertility doll, which is carved to insure beauty for the unborn child, exemplifies the ideal for the head and face.

Antubam describes the Ghanaian ideal of a beautiful neck as follows:

The neck which should have wrinkles or rings on it must fall into an elongated shape with the smaller part of it tapering towards the head. The wrinkles or rings here must be an odd number when counted to be a perfect beauty.[9]

The torso is expected to appear egg-shaped with the widest part of the oval at the neck. The egg-shaped oval is also a requirement for the thigh.

This requirement of beauty is probably what makes Ghanaian men especially like substantial thighs and buttocks. And there is the same latent principle at work, when Ghanaians even after they have been to school and passed through the Western ideal of straight and streamlined forms, still consciously or unconsciously shoot out their buttocks, when they walk, in order that they may appear beautiful. It is fascinating to watch the so-called highly educated and refined Ghanaian ladies coming out of church, making strenuous efforts to push their buttocks out to form a concave at the back of the waist in order to appear beautiful. And, their tight Western dress stresses this point, for it shows their form more clearly.[10]

Legs, too, must form egg-shaped ovals with the widest part towards the knee. Mothers of female babies tie beads at the joints of the neck base, waist, elbows, wrists, knees, and ankles in an attempt to control the development of the muscles so that they will develop ideal beauty.

America

In contrast an ideal American female form is described by Morton as follows:

The most enviable height is five feet five or six. Other characteristics of the contemporary ideal figure include an oval head and face; slender arms, tapering from wrist to elbow and very little, if any, larger at the elbow; shoulders and hips are the same width; waistline well curved; thighs the same width as the hips, tapering to gracefully proportioned calves; slender ankles and slender feet. Other characteristics in our conception of ideal proportions are a neck one-third the length of the face and not wider than the jaw; shoulders approximately three times width of the head; elbows coming to the waistline, wrists coming to one-half the height of the figure; hands the length of the face; and the width of the hands, when placed flat with fingers straight, equivalent to the widest part of the foot.[11]

Few assertions are as explicit as those made by Morton. Often the ideal can only be imputed from the negative aspect of an implied nonideal that the writer expects the reader to recognize. Thus another writer states that, "When the entire figure is above average in size, a girl will come to prefer larger sizes in everything—except patterned fabrics. In these she will probably avoid large motifs, not because they are too big for her figure, but because they create unwelcome lines," [12] The implication is that American readers, at least, will recognize that female size describable as large is not a cultural preference among Americans. The negative approach to ideals is often revealed in attention given to figure "problems." The word "overweight" refers to unattractiveness as much as to health problems for both men and women in America. However, whereas general largeness of frame may not be ideal for women, the reverse is true for men. In fact, smallness of stature, in proportion to other men, is a generally undesirable quality as far as ideal standards are concerned. Needless to say, whatever the physical attribute, it only becomes a beauty "problem" in reference to some cultural ideal. Being fat, for instance, is not defined in all cultures as an aesthetically negative quality.

Those commenting on the art of dress often suggest that an individual identify his body characteristics and modify his appearance so that he resembles the ideal. Types of body characteristics, usually negative in social value, are frequently provided so that a person can quickly identify his "problem" and relate it to a proposed solution. Names for these "problem types" vary; however, for Americans they are usually associated with deviations from average, either real or ideal, of height, weight, and figure proportions. "Problem" body types may be described as follows: tall, short, muscular, overweight, heavy, chunky, stocky, thin, out-of-proportion (large bust, round shoulders, broad shoulders, large hips). "Problems" in facial form, actually deviations from an ideal "perfect oval," are also commonly described as negative types—short square, long thin, large round, long square, pointed chin, broad forehead, and high forehead.

achieving the illusion
of ideal body form

If body form does not conform to the ideal, some cultures offer solutions that will aid in creating an illusion of beauty. An individual may be encouraged to dress himself so that he appears to have, or approaches having, ideal form. Dress for him thus becomes cultural disguise as well as an embellishment. Creating the illusion of beauty can be accomplished by hiding the body; by reconstructing parts of the body that do not measure up to standards; by attracting attention away from the part of the body that deviates from the ideal; and by optical illusion achieved through color and line combinations in dress and cosmetics, which alter appearance visually if not in actuality.

An individual can hide body surface with various items of apparel, hair growths, and cosmetics. Voluminous wrappings will conceal body form as well as surface—a loose shift or tunic creates more doubt concerning body contours than a pair of snug fitting trousers. Men's beards hide facial contours and create new shapes.

The body may be reconstructed artificially by constricting waistlines, hips, breasts, and feet with bindings, corsetry, and coverings, or in reality by diet and exercise, to approach a cultural ideal.

Contrast is a device often used to call attention to certain parts of the body, and thereby lessen attention to parts that the displayer wishes to de-emphasize. A man's white shirt and dark business suit call attention to his face through contrast of color and value. Collars and jewelry can also introduce contrasting lines and forms close to the face. The rest of the body and its costume become part of the background, and "problems" such as large hips and overweight may not be noticed.

Cosmetics and paint can also be used to divert attention. Black penciling around eyes can draw interest from other facial features. Lines and shadings made with powder, rouge, and paint can create the illusion of a different facial shape.

The use of line combinations to create illusion in dress may only be effective for those who have learned how to perceive in certain ways. If visual cues that create perspective are missing, illusion may not be created. At least studies reported by Gregory indicate that visual responses to lines are usually determined by, or greatly modified by, cultural conditioning. Westerners are highly oriented

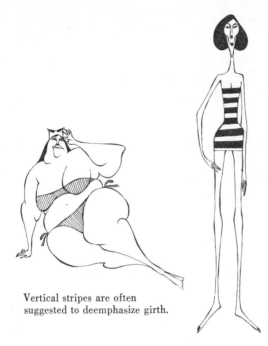

Horizontal stripes are especially suited to the need of a tall woman.

Fig. 6–10. Rules for the use of line combinations to create illusion in dress may not even be effective for those who have learned to perceive in certain ways if the rules are not applicable in all cases. (Courtesy of Robert Frisbe, *Chicago Tribune Magazine*, copyright 1967.)

Vertical stripes are often suggested to deemphasize girth.

to a world of rectangles and right angles, and to roads, railroads, and other parallel lines that converge by perspective. They are thus prepared to handle illusion in dress that results from different straight-line relationships. Zulus, however, live in what has been called a circular culture, and have no such orientation since they reside in round huts with round doors and plow in curved lines.[13]

Also line combinations must be looked at in relation to the total visual image that body and dress present. On one figure they may create one type of effect, on another figure quite a different one, hence rules cannot be arbitrarily applied even within the same culture, let alone across cultures.

summary

In all societies ideals for beauty in personal appearance develop. These include ideals for body form as well as for the dress that people wear. A society's ideals for beauty change through time, and what is an ideal appearance in one society may be very different from what is ideal in another. If body form does not measure up to the ideal, dress may be used to modify body form, hide the discrepancy, or create the illusion of the ideal.

7

THE ART OF DRESS: FORM AND MEANING

When individuals manipulate their body covering and ornament in relationship to cultural ideals they are practicing the art of dress. An individual practices the art of dress as creator, or appreciates the art of dress as viewer. As creator, his role resembles that of the sculptor, since he is concerned with three-dimensional form and therefore encounters similar problems. His media include the body itself and various materials such as metal, cloth, leather, and paint. As viewer, he contemplates the form of dress and responds to its meaning.

creating forms of dress

The body has certain plastic qualities. Hair can be straightened, curled, and forced into many different shapes. Breasts, waistlines, hips, feet, and heads can be molded by binding. Skin texture can be modified by scarring. Ears, noses, lips, and almost every conceivable body part has in some place, or at some time, been purposely redesigned by cosmetic practice or surgery, amateur or professional. Diet and exercise may also be influential in development of body form.

If the body itself does not allow full exercise of one's talent for molding, malleable metals can be converted into decorative accessories or plastics molded into desirable coverings such as boots or helmets. Flexible materials such as animal skins and furs, or those made of fibers from natural or man-made sources, have provided

Fig. 7–1. The body has certain plastic qualities; hair can be straightened, curled, and forced into many different shapes. (Courtesy of (a) the Federal Ministry of Information, Lagos, Nigeria, (b) *Vogue*, copyright 1971 by The Condé Nast Publications Inc., (c) Mary Ellen Roach, (d) Richard W. Reierson, and (e) *Vogue*, copyright 1967 by The Condé Nast Publications Inc.

(a)

(b)

man with the most widely used media of costume sculpture besides the body itself. Liquids are of minor importance in the art of dress, but often an individual's dress is completed with fluids: cosmetics or paint, as well as scents and lotions. Physically and socially dress may be a second skin; aesthetically, however, it is a second form, if form is considered to include the total combination of aesthetic elements (color, line, value, texture, shape)[1] that a costumed body presents.

Viewed aesthetically, the body has a structure of its own that can be viewed independently or as a base for presentation of a total

(c)

(d)

(e)

Fig. 7–2. As an independent structure, the body has observable shape, color, textures, value contrasts, and lines that define the total shape and consitutent shapes. (Courtesy of *Vogue*, copyright 1971 by The Condé Nast Publications Inc.)

Fig. 7–3. The body, as structural base, plus the coverings and decorations imposed upon it, provides the total effect that receives evaluation as in this example of a Fingo woman from South Africa. (Courtesy of Percy Wannerton, Rainbow Transparencies, Capetown, South Africa.)

design. Thus the impact of the aesthetic display of dress on the viewer stems from the inherent qualities (form and movement) of the human body as well as the form imposed on that body through application of external forces and materials.

As an independent structure, the body has observable shape, color, texture, value contrasts, and lines that define the total shape and constituent shapes. In its totality, the body is made up of a number of component shapes—legs, arms, head, neck, and trunk—arranged bilaterally on a vertical axis. Contrasting horizontal line direction is created by an alignment of shoulders, hips, knees, ankles, feet, eyes, mouth, and ears. Color and value contrast and texture are provided by the skin, hair, and eyes.

Changes in posture alter the visual impact of body and dress as do body movements. Both posture and movement may be greatly influenced by social customs; thus, people in different cultures may learn to stand, sit, squat, and walk in different ways. Beauty, therefore, may be recognizable only in those stances or movements characteristic of the culture.

The body, as structural base, plus the coverings and decorations imposed upon it, provides the total effect that receives aesthetic evaluation. The total effect is of significance because dress is a failure, aesthetically speaking, in any particular society if the total impression it presents is not a pleasing one.

As indicated in a discussion of ideals of beauty presented earlier, aesthetic relationships between dress and body vary: body and dress may merge, the form of dress may diverge from body form and approach independent form, or the body itself may be an independent form. Appreciation of the aesthetic qualities of the independent body form dates to prehistory—among earliest artifacts known are small carvings of nude figures. The nude condition, as an attractive alternate to the clothed state, was notable among the Greeks who "attached great importance to their nakedness," especially in the Olympic games.[2] Among some groups of people the nude body, with only jewelry, accessories, or cosmetics as embellishments, is the usual condition. In the latter case the body is dominant in the total visual effect that an individual presents and not a structural base that fades into the background. When strong moral sanctions for wearing of body coverings and against nudity exist, the nearly nude body drops out of consideration as an alternate way of presenting the human body.

Since the completely undecorated body is not the usual in any society, the body plus dress is the total form most often described in aesthetic terms. The colors, lines, shapes, value contrasts, and textures of the body and those of dress, blend to create a total form that has a unique expression of its own.

In analyzing the relationship of body and dress, typologies may be used. In Chapter Six typologies were presented that can be used cross-culturally in classifying forms of dress. These were designated as reconstructing, enclosing, and attached. DeLong's uniform-multiform and determinate-indeterminate pairs of opposite types can also be applied cross-culturally.[3] Utilizing opposite types, she describes ranges in perception as "uniform" vs. "multiform" and "determi-

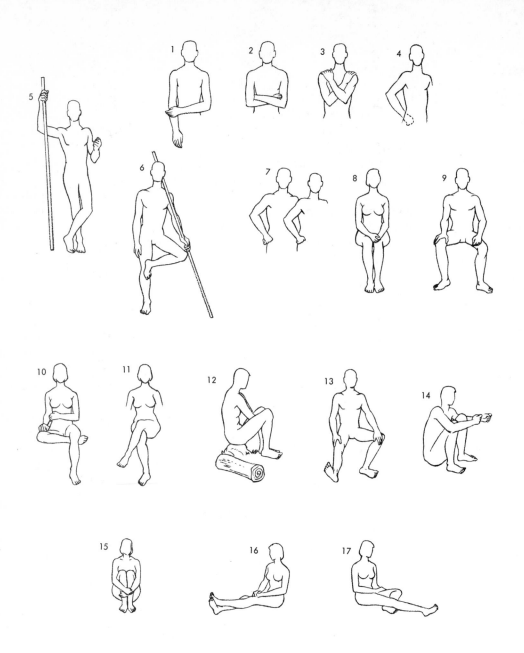

Fig. 7–4. Posture types are shown in this sampling from the classification scheme of Hewes. The figures numbered 1 and 2 are common resting positions; by contrast, the arm-on-shoulder postures of the next two figures are found mainly among western American Indians. Next (5, 6, and 7) are variations of the one-legged Nilotic stance found in the Sudan, Venezuela, and elsewhere. Chair-sitting (8, 9, 10 and 11) spread from the ancient Near East, but the Arabs there have replaced it with floor-sitting (12, 13, 14, 15, 16, and

17). Sitting cross-legged (18 and 19) predominates south and east of areas under Near Eastern influence. While sedentary kneeling postures (20, 21, 22, and 23) are typically Japanese, sitting with the legs folded to one side (24 and 25) is a feminine trait, with a rare exception being the male Mohave Indians. The deep squat (26, 27, and 28) is uncomfortable for adult Europeans, but replaces the sitting posture for at least a fourth of mankind. The last two rows show various asymmetrical postures. (Adapted from Gordon W. Hewes, "The Anthropology of Posture," *Scientific American*, February, 1957.)

Fig. 7–5. The flamenco dancer uses changes in posture and body movement to create aesthetic effects. (Courtesy of Lenore Landry.)

nate" vs. "indeterminate." Uniform and multiform designate viewing a costume in its totality versus viewing it according to its parts. The terms "determinate" and "indeterminate" describe how sharply distinguishable individually perceived parts can be.

analyzing the meaning and form of dress

Dress has meaning as well as form. The total visual effect or total form of dress can be analyzed by breaking it down into elemental aesthetic forms (colors, lines, shapes, textures, values) and describing *how* these elements are organized into particular relationships. Analyses of *meaning* are concerned with emotional responses to the form of dress and reasons *why* certain arrangements of dress may be thought more beautiful than others. The person trying to explain why some arrangement pleases more than another may consider physiological, psychological, social, cultural, and philosophical reasons; or he may apply customary belief, common sense, and personal opinion.

The terms color, line, shape, texture, and value provide a generally well-understood language for communication on matters of form, and they can be used without cultural prejudice. As descriptions of form, they can be used in comparing dress, as varied as that of a Masai, Frenchman and Nigerian, cross-culturally. On the other hand, designations of certain colors, lines, shapes, textures and values as "best" or ideal are culturally determined preferences, not necessarily applicable across cultures. Interpretations of the emotional effects of these formal elements are, therefore, concerned with meaning as well as form.

However, we cannot anticipate that all people will react to formal elements of design in the same way. To say arbitrarily that a "line may be gay and humorous, or stiff and severe" and that "it may be light and delicate or awkwardly heavy" [4] is to present only one point of view and to predict only what might be true in one cultural setting. Also the negative connotation of "awkwardly heavy" suggests a preference, hence an ideal.

The terms unity, rhythm, balance, emphasis, and proportion have been used to represent principles for organization of the art elements. However, an unambiguous principle must be a statement of relationship and not just an independent word. To say that "proportion is a principle of art" is like saying that potatoes are soup. Only when the relationship of potatoes to other ingredients in a soup is made clear is the principle of soup-making understood.

Likewise, the word "proportion" does not fully explain relationships among formal elements. To say that "good proportion aims to create a satisfactory or beautiful relationship between parts and their relationship to the whole" [5] is a move toward stating relationships. However, since the concept "good" cannot be measured in any objective way, this kind of principle can be utilized only as a philosophical statement made in relation to a cultural ideal. As a matter of fact, because of the traditional use of these terms (unity, rhythm, balance, emphasis, and proportion) in descriptions of culturally ideal relationships of art elements, as well as general difficulties in defining them without bringing in the ideal, they have only limited usefulness in objective evaluation of relationships among forms. On the whole, they are more used in, and more useful in, subjective evaluations expressive of particular points of view, reflecting either cultural ideals or unique personal perspectives.

Fig. 7–6. The terms color, line, shape, texture, and value can be used to compare dress as diverse as that of a Frenchman, a Nigerian, and a Masai. (Courtesy of (a) *Vogue*, copyright 1969 by The Condé Nast Publications Inc., (b) the Federal Ministry of Information, Lagos, Nigeria, and (c) Richard W. Reierson.)

114

Sensitivity to the difficulties involved in interpreting cultural ideals for dress for the American female is revealed in the following statement:

In selecting a hat, one will choose lines that are becoming to facial shape and features and will give better proportions to the figure. A person whose face is widest at the cheek and narrow at the forehead may wish to have trim that ends at the forehead to help make the shape more nearly oval.[6]

The authors realized the subjective nature of evaluative terms such as "becoming" and "better proportions" and the possibility of different interpretations. They, therefore, tempered the potentially dictatorial quality of their comments on how to arrive at visually satisfying arrangements of appearance by using the word "may" and suggesting *one* possible way, not *the* possible way, for achieving an attractive appearance. However, they still offer a cultural solution for a culturally defined "problem," a problem that may not be widely recognized cross-culturally. The problem they refer to is failure to measure up to a cultural ideal for shape of face: since an oval face is a traditionally perpetuated cultural ideal for the American female, they suggest how to disguise digression from that ideal.

Emotional reactions to the aesthetic qualities of dress are commonly recognized within all cultures. For example, the meaning of a particular item of dress can be identified within a specific culture; however, another culture may attach different meanings to the same thing. A veil on a Muslim woman has a religious meaning, whereas a veil on a fashionable woman in the United States has only decorative significance. Even in the same society, similar forms of dress may have different meanings.

On the other hand, different things may have the same meaning in different cultures. For example, people in different cultures have interpreted different parts of a woman's body as being sexually attractive: in Japan a woman's neck; in the United States sometimes a woman's legs, sometimes her breasts, sometimes her buttocks.

In the handling of subjective data, such as cultural meanings, which are difficult to measure with any kind of common measure, typologies are also used. Such typologies have only a limited range of application and are constructed for use in a specific social group and have meaning only for that group. For example, a typology describing bodies as stocky, overweight, thin, tall, and short has limitations as a classification system: although it appears to be a cross-culturally applicable typology of form, it really presents meanings of different body forms for only one society—American.

(a)

(b)

Fig. 7–7. Similar forms of dress have a different meaning in the same society. (Courtesy of (a) Department of Public Relations, Marquette University, and (b) Mila Schön.)

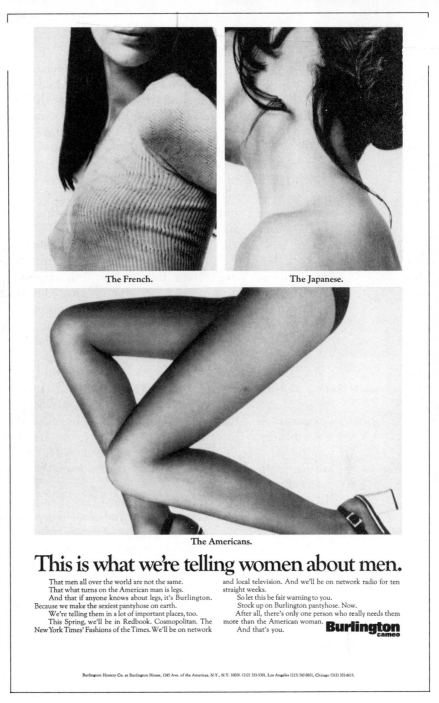

The French.   The Japanese.

The Americans.

This is what we're telling women about men.

That men all over the world are not the same.
That what turns on the American man is legs.
And that if anyone knows about legs, it's Burlington.
Because we make the sexiest pantyhose on earth.
We're telling them in a lot of important places, too.
This Spring, we'll be in Redbook. Cosmopolitan. The New York Times' Fashions of the Times. We'll be on network and local television. And we'll be on network radio for ten straight weeks.
So let this be fair warning to you.
Stock up on Burlington pantyhose. Now.
After all, there's only one person who really needs them more than the American woman.
And that's you.

Burlington cameo

Fig. 7–8. People in different cultures have interpreted different parts of a woman's body as being sexually attractive. (Courtesy of Burlington Industries, Inc.)

117

Overweight has a negative meaning for Americans, but not necessarily for people in all cultures. Some find obesity beautiful. In addition, tallness and shortness may have different connotations for men and women. This typology obviously cannot be applied to all people within a culture, let alone cross-culturally.

Other typologies go beyond the purely physical descriptions of body or facial shapes and include personality classification. In principle these typologies classify opposite types of individuals based upon their physical attributes, including height, build, coloring, and voice timbre; and non-physical characteristics, such as attitudes and emotional characteristics.

Yin and Yang is an example of a system that has been used in the United States for giving help with clothing selection. Masculine or Yang versus feminine or Yin opposites are set up as bases for evaluating personal characteristics. One delineation of the Yin-Yang system makes clear that the Yang range of possible personal characteristics has not been considered as desirable for white American women as the Yin range.[7] Some of the Yin characteristics win the culturally positive descriptions of "beautiful," "graceful," "rich and glowing," "feminine," and "youthful." However, not one Yang characteristic qualifies as "beautiful." Instead, Yang characteristics are described as "heavy," "mannish," "haughty," "strong," "muscular," "large," and "older"—terms ordinarily carrying negative cultural connotations when applied to American women, for the traditional female role has not been associated with aggressiveness and strength. In addition, the appearance of youth rather than age has been more desirable.

Other cultures have typologies, too. For example, four traditional types of women are described in India as the 1) *padmini* or lotus woman, 2) *chitrini* or art woman, 3) *samkhini* or conch woman, and 4) *hastini* or elephant woman. Each of these is characterized by certain physical and psychological attributes with the lotus woman being the most desirable and the elephant woman the least. The history of this typology in India dates to the third and fourth centuries A.D.[8]

Since it is difficult to create a typology which spans all races, some typologies have had limited usefulness even within a single culture because of an implicit racial bias.

The meaning of any typology is ordinarily shared only by the members of a culture. Therefore, typologies involving subjective evaluation of meanings of dress may be useful but should be acknowledged as generally having a utility that is limited to a cultural setting and particular time.

135 CHITRINI OR ART WOMAN
Second best

136 PADMINI OR LOTUS WOMAN
The most desirable type

137 HASTINI OR ELEPHANT WOMAN
The undesirable type

138 SHANKHINI OR CONCH WOMAN
The common type

Fig. 7–9. In traditional India four typologies of woman are described on the basis of physical and psychological characteristics. (Further information on these four categories may be found in P. Thomas, *Kāma Kalpa* or *The Hindu Ritual of Love*, published by D. B. Taraporevala Sons & Co. Private Ltd. Treasure House of Books, Bombay, India, p. 76, Fig. lix. Drawn after finds at Begram, 2nd century A.D.)

summary

Forms of dress are describable in aesthetic terms; they also have meanings. The aesthetic characteristics of dress are always seen in relation to the body, for an item of dress is really a part of dress only when it is viewed in relationship to the body. The total visual effect of dress can be analyzed by describing its aesthetic components; that is, the colors, lines, shapes, textures, and values, that body and dress present.

The degree to which the organization of these elements is judged to approach the beautiful depends upon the society in which evaluations are being made, for evaluations are made in relation to cultural ideals which prescribe the preferred or most desirable appearance for a particular society. These ideals depict the desirable rather than the achievable and may not be relevant for all segments of a particular society.

8

THE INDIVIDUAL AND THE ART OF DRESS

H ow people "practice" the art of dress is influenced both by their culture and by personal preferences. Variety in forms of dress in any society is limited by the materials available, the type of technology, and social values. Some societies allow much more leeway in aesthetic expression through dress than do others. In one, possible varieties of dress are prescribed within very narrow limits. In another, relatively little social control is exercised, and individualism may even be encouraged. Thus a man in an American Amish community may have choices between only two styles of coat jackets, one for ordinary wear and one for special services. American men of other religious persuasions may choose among several basic styles of jackets and a variety of fabrics, designs, colors, and textures. Thus each individual practices the art of dress within the limits established by his social group. If he does not wish to act within the limits set by his group, he may withdraw from the group, provided sanctions are not too strong, other groups of affiliation are available, or the isolation of uniqueness not intolerable.

In this chapter we will discuss the general nature of cultural standards for dress, how individuals act in relation to cultural standards, and how cultural standards become conventionalized into canons of "good taste."

cultural standards
for the art of dress

Cultural standards provide order in people's lives since they enable individuals to adopt modes of behavior from a limited range of possibilities rather than from an infinite number of conceivable behaviors. As Benedict observes:

In culture . . . we must imagine a great arc on which are ranged the possible interests provided either by the human age-cycle or by the environment or by man's various activities. A culture that capitalized even a considerable proportion of these would be as unintelligible as a language that used all the clicks, all the glottal stops, all the labials, dentals, sibilants, and gutturals from voiceless to voiced and from oral to nasal. Its identity as a culture depends upon the selection of some segments of this arc.[1]

Cultural standards for dress limit the number of forms from which selections can be made and thereby limit a person's practice of the art of dress. Underlying adherence to cultural standards for dress is desire for social acceptance, although individuals may not be consciously aware of this desire. They may, however, be aware of social discomfort when their dress is far different from that of others in their group.

Within the group itself words like "appropriate," "proper," or "in good taste" express approval of dress. Individuals who wear the appropriate display in dress feel comfortable and accepted. However, circumstances may influence whether display in dress is judged inappropriate for wear and likely to cause social discomfort. An outsider, for example, is often excused from usual social customs in dress, especially when the insiders realize the outsider does not know the rules.

change in cultural standards

But cultural standards do not mean absence of change; instead change is inevitable. Within Western fashion history the regular abandoning of one set of standards for beautiful and appropriate dress and the establishing of new standards illustrate how change constantly occurs. Some individuals act as leaders who instigate deviations and the reformulation of standards; others, who are not innovators, are still sensitive to change and register their sensitivity by either encouraging or discouraging it, thereby earning for themselves labels such as "conservative" or "liberal." However, such is the persistence of change in standards for beautiful dress, that the conservative as well as the liberal eventually capitulates. It is both individualistic and socially conforming to follow changes in standards; for, "paradoxically, you can't stay yourself unless you change yourself skillfully with the fashion." [2] To be himself within a world of shifting standards for beauty of dress, the individual must be, consciously or unconsciously, constantly checking and cross-referencing to see what is culturally valid and how he can maintain an attractive self-type within the limits of what is culturally valid.

factors influencing choice of dress

An individual's interpretations of the art of dress are based on his understanding of cultural standards; however, personal preferences may intervene. Thus he may lean heavily toward conformity with prescribed dress or he may strain for individuality.

Societal Types

In a traditional society ruled by custom, an individual is limited in his dress by age, sex, and perhaps occupation. In industrial societies, an individual may have many alternatives: in addition to age and sex differences in dress, a wide variety of occupations exists as well as a multitude of leisure-time activities that require specialized

(a)

(b)

Fig. 8–1. Although separated by an ocean, Black Panthers in America and IRA women in Northern Ireland wear berets and dark glasses to express group affiliation. (Courtesy of (a) Photoreporters, and Pressens Bild, Stockholm, Sweden,) and (b) Claus C. Meyer for Black Star.)

dress. In such a society, the individual may accept the cultural standards of dress (the dominant fashion of the time) or may reject them and replace them with those of a subcultural group with whom he affiliates or with his own idiosyncratic preferences. The complexities of industrial society allow the existence of many subgroups with divergent and even contradictory belief systems which may contain strong beliefs about dress that limit individualism. These subgroups include ones with strong political, religious, and social philosophies, such as Castro and his followers, the Black Panthers, the Amish, the Hasidim, various Catholic orders, and youth groups of our contemporary world.

Fig. 8–2. Strong religious beliefs may limit individualism in dress. The Amish have long practiced restraint in dress. (Courtesy of John Launois for Black Star.)

Fig. 8–3. Social philosophy may limit individualism in dress. Youth groups may choose worn denims as indicative of their social philosophy. (Courtesy of Richard Sharpe.)

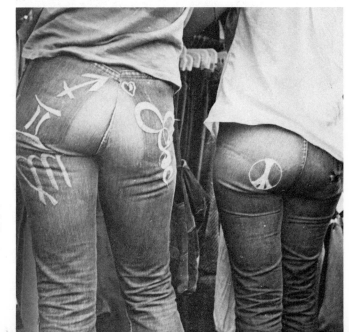

The Quakers are an historical example of a group who, in an earlier time, prescribed dress within carefully defined limits of aesthetic expression. They rejected the ornamental aspects of dress, which were considered unnecessary, along with ornamentation in speech, manners, architecture, and house furnishings. The early Friends dressed in a plain version of the everyday dress of the time but stripped of superfluous ornaments. Later the "plain dress" became standardized into almost a Quaker uniform: "the broad-brimmed hat and lapel-less 'shadbelly' coat, the coal-scuttle bonnet and cap, the plain shawl and dove-gray gown." [3] The emphasis on plainness was not confined to Quakers but was part of the Protestant taste of the seventeenth century, a counterreaction to the extremely elaborate baroque style associated with the counter-Reformation.[4] An individual who subscribed to the beliefs of the Quakers subordinated his desire for individual distinction to the group's regulations.

Another example, drawn from a very different social context, are the geishas of Japan, who have some aspects of a subcultural group with strong traditions in their dress. The kimono symbolizes the differentiation of the seasons and each geisha, like every Japanese woman, is expected to conform to the tradition of wearing a kimono

Fig. 8–4. This "maiki" (young geisha-to-be) is dressed in a traditional silk kimono. The elaborate obi is tied in a special bow, which drapes and flows loosely down the back. Only maikos or dancing girls wear their obi (cumberbund) tied in this manner. Usually obi are tied in the "drum" or "butterfly" style (for a young girl) which is easily distinguished from the style worn by the entertainers. Long-flowing sleeves worn by the maiko or by brides during the Japanese wedding ceremony are called "furisode." (Courtesy of Japan Air Lines.)

that has a decorative motif appropriate to the season in which she is wearing it. She must not wear a kimono decorated with chrysanthemums in spring or cherry blossoms in the fall.[5] In addition, sleeve length and the tying of the obi are special marks of the geisha.

Toffler in *Future Shock* contrasts the American businessman's garb with that of a motorcyclist subgroup and explains that the selection of a life-style narrows choices for the individual in either case:

The American male who wears a button down collar and garter-length socks probably also wears wing-tip shoes and carries an attache case. If we look closely, chances are we shall find a facial expression and brisk manner intended to approximate those of the stereotypical executive. The odds are astronomical that he will not let his hair grow wild in the manner of rock musician Jimi Hendrix. He knows, as we do, that certain clothes, manners, forms of speech, opinions and gestures hang together, while others do not. He may know this only by "feel," or "intuition," having picked it up by observing others in the society, but the knowledge shapes his actions.

The black-jacketed motorcyclist who wears steel-studded gauntlets and an obscene swastika dangling from his throat completes his costume with rugged boots, not loafers or wing-tips. He is likely to swagger as he walks and to grunt as he mouths his antiauthoritarian platitudes. For he, too, values consistency. He knows that any trace of gentility or articulateness would destroy the integrity of his style.[6]

Thus as specific individuals in any culture make choices in dress, they are subject to constraints. When an individual enjoys the art of dress, achieving personal distinction from others in his group of associates may become a challenge for him. As he makes conscious clothing selections and manipulates and interprets fashion details, he may see himself as having achieved individuality. Those people outside the group, however, may view him and others in his group as looking alike, even identical in dress; for the outsiders are not usually sensitive to the details important within the group. Thus American youth who value individuality in appearance may not look individual to outsiders, although within their group individual distinctions are recognized.

Occupational Choice

Some people are constrained in their individuality in dress because their occupations have rigid dress codes. Occupational requirements for dress may restrict individuals when the clothing is functionally

Fig. 8–5. People outside the group view individuals within the group as looking alike, even identical; for the outsiders are not usually sensitive to the details important within the group. (Courtesy of Richard Sharpe.)

Fig. 8–6. American youth who value individuality in appearance may not look individual to outsiders, although within their group individual distinctions are recognized. (Courtesy of Richard Sharpe.)

Fig. 8–7. Masai warriors may look alike to outsiders not sensitive to details of dress that differentiate them from each other. (Courtesy of Richard W. Reierson.)

mandatory as in the case of fire fighters or workers in danger of being exposed to radiation. Occupational dress which is also utilitarian but not functionally mandatory is exemplified by uniforms of individuals in the service trades and professions, such as hairdressers, barbers, cooks, maids, mechanics, doctors, and nurses. Although not strictly necessary for the job, the uniform saves the individual's regular wardrobe which is usually more expensive and less expendable than work clothing. Occupational dress is required in other cases for symbolic reasons such as easy identification of soldiers, police, stewardesses, and railroad conductors.

By contrast, individuals in other types of occupations without many constraints in dress have more chance to express individuality. Those who especially appear to have freedom of expression in their dress are entertainers. Sometimes entertainers who become well-known are individualistic at first but after they are copied by others no longer maintain distinctiveness. Greta Garbo is a case in point. One observer comments that in the 1930s and 1940s, Garbo wore a sweater, trousers, dark glasses, and Van Dyck hat and was recognized everywhere. Furthermore he states:

(a)

(b)

Fig. 8–8. When in uniform, both West Point graduates and Nigerian police display little individuality. (Courtesy of (a) Culver Pictures, Inc., and (b) the Federal Ministry of Information, Lagos, Nigeria.)

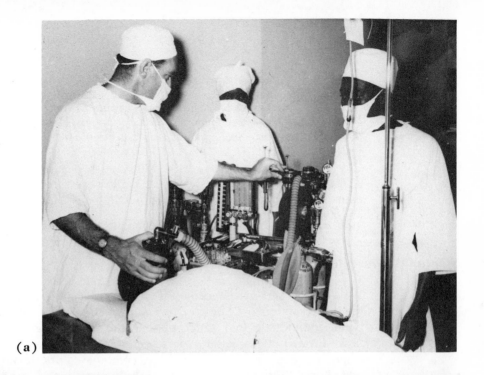

(a)

(b)

(c)

Fig. 8–9. Occupational uniforms limit individuality in dress as shown by a Nigerian medical team, a Spanish waiter, and a Kenyan gamekeeper. (Courtesy of (a) the Federal Ministry of Information, Lagos, Nigeria, (b) Lenore Landry, and (c) Richard W. Reierson.)

. . . She was, in fact, the first beatnik. She loved to bathe naked off the rocks at the Antibes.

Now, she dresses with the same air but the world has caught up with her and her style is no longer outstanding. Last time she was shopping with a friend in Chelsea only one man realized who she was and he was an antique dealer.[7]

An array of pictures of Garbo in the thirties shows her in various pants outfits which do not look distinctive today but were innovative and avante-garde at that time.

Personal Characteristics and Preferences

Well-known personalities like Greta Garbo are easily visible when they dress uniquely; however, every person is unique in some way. Some individuals find great pleasure in expressing their uniqueness through dress, others do not. Some individuals in societies where freedom in dress is possible, combine colors, textures, lines, and shapes to display their aesthetic responses, moods, and feelings. The individual can take into account his body characteristics (such as coloring and body build), his self-image, and his preferences in dress to differentiate himself from others; for dress serves as a

Fig. 8–10. A picture of Garbo in the thirties shows her in a pants outfit which does not look distinctive today but was innovative and avant-garde at that time. (Courtesy of Culver Pictures, Inc.)

stimulus for aesthetic responses from other people. In addition, response is expected from the displayer of dress since the displayer can respond to his own creations on the basis of what he has learned from others. Because an observer receives only external cues concerning the inner emotional state that prompted a display of dress that he observes, he can only imagine what the aesthetic emotion experienced by the displayer is like. However, he has opportunity to register another kind of aesthetic emotion—that resulting from contemplation. For displayer and observer alike the subject for contemplation is an arrangement of the human body, which has its own aesthetic qualities, into some kind of visual relation with materials of different colors, textures, shapes, and dimensions. Reactions to the three-dimensional, mobile display achieved are seldom on the basis of its aesthetic nature alone, since pure aesthetic acts of creating and contemplating dress are virtually impossible. Incentives to communicate various social and psychological states via beauty in

Fig. 8–11. An individual's dress may create or contribute to the maintenance of mood, as in the case of college students in the United States protesting the Viet Nam War. (Courtesy of John Brubaker.)

Fig. 8–12. The wrapping of the Ethiopian *shamma* indicates the mourners' mood of sadness. (Courtesy of Carl K. Eicher.)

dress invariably develop and overlap with and modify the aesthetic expression. Adornment, therefore, usually carries several messages, those that are aesthetic and those of various kinds of social and psychological significance.

Dress relates to subjective states called mood. Mood can be identified by pairs of contrasting adjectives which suggest opposite emotional states, with a range of possible intermediate states between them. Thus happy-gloomy, cheerful-melancholy, good humored-cross, anxious-content, retiring-assertive suggest polar states of mood in the English language. An individual's dress may create mood, contribute to maintenance of mood, indicate change in mood, or may disguise mood.

Feelings about modesty in dress, the importance of personal display or the value of thrift can also be indicated by an individual through his choice of clothing.[8]

taste in dress

Some individuals attempt to achieve a measure of individuality through exercise of taste. In highly complex societies, or in levels of society where many choices are available and acts of discrimination among alternative forms of dress are commonplace, choosing the appropriate may be regarded as exercise of taste. Exercise of taste is characteristic of members of the dominant class who frequently occupy themselves with pleasure, consumption, and display to affirm their rank and personal worth, thereby imposing a constant concern with fashions and the qualities of refined or precious objects upon others.[9] One writer says it is no accident

. . . that the term for discrimination in art, dress and conduct should be the name of one of the senses. . . . It is rooted in the formal analogy of taste in food with taste in aesthetic and social objects. Taste is the "choosing" sense. . . . of immediate and unreflecting judgments of the acceptable and unacceptable. Governing the admission or rejection of food, it makes no intermediate discriminations but only absolute decisions.[10]

Taste, therefore, is the general orientation of an individual that results in his making judgments about the aesthetic quality and social appropriateness of cultural products—nonmaterial as well as material. Thus judgments of taste can be directed toward music, manners, and social conduct as well as paintings, sculpture, and dress. In addition, taste is exhibited within a social context and is judged in relation to standards for taste that have grown out of the behavior patterns of the social group. An individual's taste is a measure of his ability to live up to a group standard.

Fig. 8–13. An individual's taste is a measure of his or her ability to live up to a group standard. (Courtesy of Richard Sharpe.)

We may say that taste operates at a social-psychological level because judgments are applied to an *individual's* pattern of selection from the alternatives open to him, but he is judged on the basis of how well his choices measure up to *group* levels. In other words he is assessed in regard to his ability to differentiate "good" from "bad" as measured against arbitrary standards possessed by the group.

Taste in dress is related to the existence of a range of alternatives from which choices can be made along with the quality of rarity, or uniqueness, ascribed to some of the alternative forms available. If alternative forms are not available, or everyone possesses the same forms of dress, then everyone has "good taste," and no such thing as taste exists for no comparison can be made. If some forms of dress are scarce or rare, perhaps because only a few wealthy or prestigious people can obtain them—designer clothes or chinchilla coats, for example—more value may be placed on them as means of reinforcing the personal prestige and social value of those who can choose them.

the judges
and leaders of taste

Within a society, evaluations of taste in clothing are understood only if it is known which group norms are operating as the basis for an evaluation. When the one who judges comes from the same social stratum as the individual whose clothing is being judged, and if he has not been socialized to "outgroup" values through education, or some other means, his judgments may favor the mode of behavior within the stratum. When the judges come from different strata, very different judgments are to be predicted.

Within American society, standards for taste in dress are hard to describe since taste can be defined at many different social levels. Nevertheless, in America the types of individuals who assume *leadership* in setting taste and, more importantly, seem to be "given the right" to define "good taste" are identifiable—designers, professional critics, well-known "exhibitors," retail store buyers, and informal opinion leaders. By the act of creating some unique quality in his designs, a designer may help set the direction for taste in dress. What he creates cannot be completely idiosyncratic since his existence as a designer depends on the acceptance and use of his designs by others. As he gives support to certain trends in design and rejects others, he is serving as a critic of taste. Other critics or commentators on design of apparel make a profession of defining taste: they include writers on clothing selection or etiquette, fashion columnists for newspapers and magazines, and the committee for the Best-Dressed List and the Fashion Hall of Fame.[11] Only some exhibitors (consumers) of dress exert leadership in taste on a society-wide basis. Those who do must have highly visible ways to exhibit their dress and must have enough wealth to afford items of dress that can be measured in terms of taste. Widespread visibility occurs in certain kinds of life circumstances: some people are born into well-known families, others are in high public office or are related to individuals who are in high public office. The President of the United States and members of his family hence are potential leaders in taste although not everyone in their position has played this role. Among people who have gained public attention through combinations of achievement and personal characteristics are those in the theater, motion pictures, television, and sports. Those in the latter group are often charismatic leaders whose personal charisma frequently extends to influence in clothing.

Retail buyers also help determine taste by making selections from which their customers in turn must make selections. In addition, among the masses there are informal opinion leaders who influence choice-making of relatives, friends, and acquaintances. Their influence is exerted in face-to-face situations in the neighborhood or small community gatherings.

summary

Every day people around the world make decisions about what to wear. In all cultures, people are tutored by others who teach implicitly and explicitly what the ideals of beauty and standards for dress are. As we have seen, universal rules for achieving beautiful dress cannot be formulated, for cultural differences, the passage of time, and individual interpretations of taste intervene.

Individuals vary in the freedom they exercise in choosing their dress. Some individuals subscribe to ideologies of groups that narrowly prescribe what dress should be; others value having great leeway in dress and exhibit a variety of forms of dress; still others submit to some restraints in dress, for example, wearing uniforms for work. In complex societies, practical problems arise for individuals who see many alternatives of dress facing them. Selecting a life-style may narrow choices; thus the businessman or the individual in the youth commune chooses from among only a narrow range of items.

9

DRESS AND
THE ARTS

Dress, whether covering and ornamenting of the body for work, play, or special ceremonies, may be viewed as an art form in itself or as an integral part of the performing, visual, and literary arts.

dress as a decorative art

Examples from all over the world illustrate how the body can be converted into a decorative object: the Tchikrin of Central Brazil decorate with body paint, the Tiv of Nigeria with scars; women in the United States arrange their hair in intricate designs with the

Fig. 9–1. The Tchikrin of Brazil decorate with body paints. (Courtesy of Claudia Andujar, *National History Magazine.*)

Fig. 9–2. The Tiv of Northern Nigeria decorate with scars. (Courtesy of the Federal Ministry of Information, Lagos, Nigeria.)

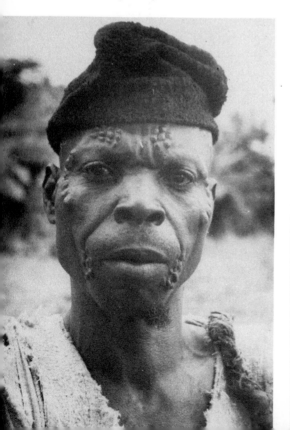

Fig. 9–3. The body may be a base for displaying ornamental coverings, jewels, and accessories. (Courtesy of *Vogue*, copyright 1968 by The Condé Nast Publications Inc.)

aid of lotions and sprays. In addition the body may be a base for displaying ornamental coverings, jewels, and accessories.

As ornamenting the body is emphasized, without regard to utility, it becomes a decorative art. This type of artistic expression was seen in dress designs included in the 1925 Paris Exhibition of Decorative and Industrial Arts. Since then Veronesi and others have recorded the contributions of European high fashion to the decorative arts.[1] In the United States the Costume Institute of the Metropolitan Museum of Art and the Museum of Contemporary Crafts of the American Craftsmen's Council have exhibited dress as an art form. But the rapidly changing shape of dress in Western fashion is not the only level on which dress is an art. Cross-cultural examples include the Court dragon robes of pre-revolutionary China and the highly decorated Japanese kimonos.

dress as an
integral part of the arts

Dress is a complement to all the arts: performing, visual, and literary. The performing arts include theatre, dance, cinema, television and music; the visual arts, painting and sculpture; the literary arts, novels, drama, short stories, and poetry.

We shall include both classical and popular forms of the arts in this analysis of dress and the arts; thus the cinema, circus, burlesque, "rock" groups, blues and country music groups are as important in our analysis as traditional art forms like opera, classical ballet, or Shakespearean drama. We also review the role of costume in the visual and literary arts.

similarities between
stage costume and everyday dress

Similarities exist between costume used in the performing arts and dress worn in everyday situations. In all life situations, dress can enhance the credibility of the individual in regard to his basic social categories of age, sex, and occupation; sometimes it indicates personality characteristics. Appropriate clothing for age and sex is utilized in everyday life to establish social and personal characteristics in first encounters. Similarly, in the theatre, dance, opera, movies, television and the circus, credibility is necessary when the performer first appears. The success of the performance, which spans a brief period of time, requires that the audience understand as many basic facts about the individual performers as costuming and make-up allow—what can be understood by being seen need not be said. Costuming that is effective must communicate ideas quickly and efficiently. As one costumer has said:

When the curtain rises, the spectator's first impression is of the costumes before his eye takes in the set or his mind registers the meaning of the lines. And throughout the action the costumes contribute to his understanding not only of the characters but of the play, in the same way that clothes help us to form our judgments of people and occasions in everyday life.[2]

142

Another way in which dress in the performing arts is similar to everyday apparel is that it is used to indicate differences among individuals as to social rank. An audience makes distinctions as they compare and contrast the costumes of performers.

special requirements
of stage costume

The differences between dress used in the performing arts and in daily life appear to be more numerous than the similarities. A performer's dress must create a visual impression that will support or supplement his performance; but, strangely enough, his dress may not be the same dress the audience would expect him to wear if the scenes were real life scenes.

Accommodation to Body Action
and Demands of Theater Life

Theatrical costume must allow for body movement and comfort. We often assume that everyday clothing accommodates the physical movements of bodies and is comfortable. In point of fact, the reverse is often true; and some individuals for the sake of fashion or

Fig. 9–4. Toe shoes allowed the ballerina to rise off the ground, "defying the laws of gravity." (Courtesy of Culver Pictures, Inc.)

personal vanity are willing to endure apparel that is too tight, too long, too small, or sometimes too large. In the performing arts, two factors are involved that necessitate particular attention to the construction of clothing in relation to body comfort and movement. First, the performers are on view to an audience and must be physically mobile and active without embarrassment. Size and fit of their garments are important, for too tight trousers may rip, too large shoes may cause stumbling. Second, in some of the performing arts, such as the dance or the circus, special designs are created to meet the extraordinary requirements made of clothing as performers move, stretch, twist, and turn their bodies. The costumes worn by ballet dancers, as an example, are designed to allow extra length at the waist for rise and fall of the chest when stretching the arms, and armholes and sleeves are set high.[3] Total length of garments also affects mobility. Only since the time when ballerinas began to wear short tutus that allowed great freedom in body movement have female ballet dancers been able to compete in dancing brilliance with their male counterparts. Moreover, a special development in ballet, dancing on points, was possible only with the creation of special blocked toe shoes. They serve as physical extensions of the body that allow the dancer " . . . to defy the laws of gravity, so to speak, by rising off the ground on the toes and thus to create an illusion of an ethereal being differing from the rest of us earthbound humans." [4] Thus, portrayals of mystical creatures and disembodied spirits, such as in *La Sylphide*, are easier for dancers who can perform on their toes.

The dress used in modern dance, however, is quite opposite to the prescribed dress of ballet that supports equally prescribed classic movements. Isadora Duncan, for example, danced in bare feet and Grecian-type flowing costumes which, except for their length, freed the body.

Comfort and adaptation to body action are important in stage costume, but sturdiness is also required. One costumer stated the general requirements as follows:

> . . . *as it is not desirable to drop flowers, sleeves and other parts of the costume while on stage, strong stitching is advisable. Two or three large hooks and eyes should be placed where most needed, speed and security being indispensable. It may be necessary to dress quickly before a performance; time is limited between the acts, and all actors are possessed of a mad desire to get out of the theatre as quickly as possible afterward.*[5]

Circus clothing was noted by one circus costumer as needing especially sturdy construction, as well as glamour, for

Fig. 9–5. Isadora Duncan danced in bare feet and Grecian-type flowing costumes which freed the body. (Courtesy of Culver Pictures, Inc.)

> *Circus costumes take a hard beating and are exposed to more elements than the usual theatrical wardrobe . . . They are packed and unpacked hundreds of times during the tour.*
>
> *Headdresses with enormous plumes and feathers must have a look of fantasy during the show, but they must pack quickly and easily. Every feather is wired to protect it from breaking.*[6]

Performers in musical extravaganzas also wear intricate headdresses which must be stored between performances as well as hold up from performance to performance.

Fig. 9–6. Performers in musical extravaganzas wear intricate headdresses. (Courtesy of Culver Pictures, Inc.)

Adjustment to
Theatre Space and Lighting

Theatre costume design can alleviate problems in effective communication created by distance between audience and performer. Some aspects of dress can be exaggerated in order that viewers from the second balcony, or highest bleachers in the circus tent, can see and understand their symbolism. For example, if all members of a theatre audience, seated anywhere from ten to seventy feet away from the stage, are to perceive an actress as "small town" and not a "city sophisticate," her costume must be exaggerated in its design.[7] Fine details are unnecessary for they will go unnoticed, or not be seen by many members of the audience. Exaggeration in circus and opera costume is even more mandatory since frequently the distance between opera and circus performers and audience members is even greater than in theatre productions.

Lighting effects make possible a much wider range of color combinations in costumes on the stage than in everyday wear. Most custom allows everyday clothing is seen under natural light or manmade light which simulates natural light.[8] Natural light isolates color whereas the colored illumination used for the stage tends to blend colors. Thus, on stage, colors not usually worn together and colors stronger in intensity than what is worn daily may be utilized. In addition, lighting may in some cases actually be a part of costuming, for the color of an outfit may be created or varied by lighting. Certain iridescent effects can be seen only under special lighting conditions.

The Performer
in Relation to His Costume

Successful portrayal of a role depends often on an individual's costume and make-up. Charlie Chaplin is a classic example of someone who successfully used costume to support his character portrayal. As one writer comments:

Imagine Charlie Chaplin in any outfit than his own . . . Much thought and experiment went into its creation. Have you ever noticed how this artist wears his shabby, droll, almost pathetic costume and how he uses it to play upon your feelings? His work is an illustrious example of a great artist's use of costume.[9]

Compatibility between the design of costume and how an artist perceives his role can give him confidence in his portrayal of that role. If he sees his costume as symbolic of the role he is playing, his identification with the role is enhanced. On the other hand, if his costume does not coincide with his visual conception of that role, he is likely to suffer confusion and discomfort as he tries to coordinate role with symbol. Lawrence Langner, founder of The Theatre Guild and American Shakespeare Festival Theatre at Stratford, Connecticut, claimed that "actors and actresses, and especially actresses, feel uncomfortable and unable to perform properly if they are antagonistic to the clothes they are wearing." [10] This antagonism may be caused by a conscious or unconscious feeling that a costume is not appropriate for the role being played. On occasion it is the result of personal vanity: the actor who wants to enhance what he considers his most attractive features and minimize others, may react negatively to a costume that he does not feel serves this purpose.

Costume can put an actor in the mood to portray a character. Dustin Hoffman commented about the make-up used for his char-

Fig. 9–7. Charlie Chaplin successfully used costume to support his character portrayal. (Courtesy of Culver Pictures, Inc.)

Fig. 9–8. Costume and make-up can put an actor in the mood to portray a character. (Photograph of Dustin Hoffman, courtesy of the actor's agent, Peter Schub, New York.)

acterization of a 121-year-old man in the movie *Little Big man,* "I defy anybody to put that make-up on and not feel old." [11] Costume and make-up can also help create a mood that actor and audience can share, and indicate change in mood. If mood is to be established convincingly, gesture, body stance, voice tones, music, and costume must complement each other, for a nonharmonious detail may result in failure to establish the desired mood.

The color of a costume is a quality that is often manipulated in efforts to create mood. In American theatre bright, contrasting colors, sharp differences in lightness and darkness are conventionally used to stress activity and gaiety, dull and dark colors to emphasize mystery or sadness.

For certain theatrical roles, the costume or make-up has become so much a part of the character that the two become intertwined and inseparable, thus the essence of a character *is* the clothing for certain roles. The traditional characters of "Harlequin," "Pierrot and Pierrette," "Peter Pan," "Mary Poppins," and "Mickey Mouse" have such definite costume requirements that the character is immediately recognizable because of the specific costume worn. The costumes for characters in the Japanese No Drama and Kabuki theatre are further examples; the costume is the character and the actor merely the "machinery" for giving the character movement.

Fig. 9–9. Traditional characters like Mickey Mouse have such definite costume requirements that the character is immediately recognizable because of the costume worn. (© Walt Disney Productions.)

The epitome of integration of dress and role occurs in the case of these stereotyped characters; indeed, the stereotyped role may constrain the actor's freedom to be innovative and curtail his personal interpretation of a role.

Relation of Costume to Type of Performance

Costume varies greatly from one performing art to another. Each type of performance seems to demand a specific type of costume.

THE MUSICAL PERFOR-MANCE The type of music produced appears related to the type of dress worn by a musical performer. For example, the formal evening dress of a symphony orchestra or a chamber group has come to be associated with the formal structure of its music; the informal and spontaneous type of music produced by jazz musicians is usually typified by casual dress. However, even among these musicians, dis-

Fig. 9–10. The formal evening dress of a chamber music group has come to be associated with the formal structure of its music. (Courtesy of Information Services, Michigan State University.)

tinctions in dress can be found. For example, compare the formal attire of the Modern Jazz Quartet with the informal attire of Dizzy Gillespie and Thelonius Monk.

The dress of singers also symbolizes the type of music they specialize in. Concert singers like Martina Arroyo and Leontyne Price often wear formal evening dress while folk-singers like Joan Baez or rock singers like Rita Coolidge use casual or flamboyant dress. The associations between dress of musicians and the type of music they produce are so stereotyped that it is difficult to imagine Gordon Lightfoot in white tie and tails or the Boston Symphony Orchestra in jeans and T-shirts.

Fig. 9–11. It is difficult to imagine Gordon Lightfoot performing in white tie and tails. (Courtesy of John Brubaker.)

Fig. 9–12. Concert singers often wear formal evening dress while folk and rock singers dress casually, as shown in the photographs on p. 151. (Courtesy of (a) Thea Dispeker, (b) and (c) John Brubaker.)

(a)

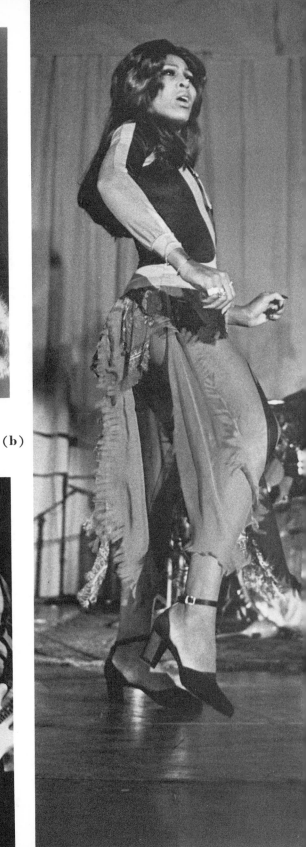

(b)

(c)

Fig. 9–13. A "gay nineties" look has become the typical dress of the singing groups known as barbershop quartets. (Courtesy of Mary Ellen Roach.)

THE GROUP PERFOR- MANCE

In many areas of music and in some forms of dance the visible presence of an individual performer is subordinated to the group. A uniform costume is one means of subordinating the individual to the group effort. Visible lack of individuality helps the audience to assess the performance as a group effort and at the same time reminds the performer that he is submitting his virtuosity to a group endeavor. In choirs, choruses, orchestras, dance lines, concert and marching bands, uniform dress is typical. The members of a choir wear choir robes, the symphony orchestra performers, formal dress. In each case, individuality of a single performer is intentionally downplayed, except for soloists or special performers who are featured against the background of the group.

In the case of the Rockettes in Radio City Music Hall, precision dancing is the trademark. Identical costumes emphasize the precision of the dance steps and create an illusion of uniformity of execution among the dancers.

Fig. 9–14. A uniform costume is one means of subordinating the individual to the group effort. (Courtesy of Information Services, Michigan State University.)

Fig. 9–15. The Rockettes' identical costumes emphasize precision of dance steps. (Courtesy of Radio City Music Hall Rockettes—Impact Photos.)

FANTASY   Some of the performing arts use a modicum of reality but strict adherence to reality is unnecessary or may even hinder achievement of a performer's artistic goal. In musicals, for example, reality is not always a desired goal, instead fantasy may be the major consideration. If the production requires a fairy-tale effect, adherence to reality may interfere. Cowboys in the musical *Oklahoma* are usually costumed in colorful shirts rather than the drab shirt of the frontier.

Productions known as "extravaganzas," such as Ziegfeld Follies or the Folies Bergères, also have ignored reality and emphasized fantasy in their costume. Fanciful dress may be created from feathers, beads, and sequins in an effort to create a costume which diverges as much as possible from the everyday. Burlesque and vaudeville performers may also appear in "unreal" costumes.

Fig. 9–16. Productions known as extravaganzas such as the Ziegfeld follies, ignored reality and emphasized fantasy in their costume. (Courtesy of Culver Pictures, Inc.)

DANCE

In classical ballet, symmetry of movement and symmetry in dress and hairdo are emphasized in order to support the formal nature of the dance. In modern dance on the other hand, free-form costumes that enhance, or become part of spontaneous, unrestrained movement are often used, and freedom to wear any type of costume that supports the underlying theme of the dance is stressed.

Fig. 9–17. In classical ballet symmetry of movement and symmetry in dress and hairdo are emphasized in order to support the formal nature of the dance. (Courtesy of Culver Pictures, Inc.)

Fig. 9–18. In modern dance costume supports spontaneous, unrestrained movement. (Courtesy of John Brubaker.)

visual and literary arts

Artists who paint or draw, create sculpture, or write literature, whether poetry, novels, or short stories, often express the emotions, personality, and social characteristics of their subjects through dress.

Visual Arts

In the visual arts costume may reflect current fashion or glorify personages painted. Until the introduction of photography, sculpture and painting were major ways of recording historical events and portraying the unique appearance of individuals. On the one hand, some artists portrayed costume of common folk and aristocrats with accuracy. Such paintings can be used for documentation of the period. On the other hand, some artists who painted portraits of the wealthy and powerful enhanced their appearance with elaborate costumes lest their importance and prestige not be fully appreciated. Since classic times derivatives of the Greek himation have been used in art works to clothe figures with honor and respect: Greek and Roman scholars were portrayed in the himation; the figure of Christ has been traditionally depicted in the same way, a sculpture of George Washington shows him in a classic pose clad in the himation.

Fig. 9–19. Since classical times, portraits of honored men have shown them clad in a version of the Greek himation. A sculpture by Horatio Greenough, 1840, shows George Washington dressed in the himation. (Courtesy of the Smithsonian Institution.)

Fig. 9–20. Paintings may be used to document the dress and adornment of either common people or aristocracy as in the case of these two sixteenth century paintings, "The Wedding Dance" by Bruegel, and the "Portrait of Federico, Prince of Urbino at the Age of Two Years," by Baroccio. (Courtesy of the Detroit Institute of Arts.)

Formal portraits of Western rulers have often shown similar archaisms. Louis XIV, for example, is portrayed in costume that mixes seventeenth-century details of dress (a full-bottomed wig, red-heeled shoes, and lace neckcloth) with sixteenth-century trunkhose.

Literary Arts

In literature, descriptions of dress usually depict for the reader the type of individual the author is creating, his social background and perhaps mood. The literary arts can document style and fashions current at the time of the writing.

Fiction writers of both short stories and novels develop characters by describing their dress and ornamentation as well as by providing appropriate dialogue for them. In *Madame Bovary*, the appearance of gentlemen at a ball was depicted by Flaubert in such a way that the reader easily picks up clues about their social standing.

Their clothes, better made, seemed of finer cloth, and their hair, brought forward in curls towards the temples, glossy with more delicate pomades. They had the complexion of wealth—that clear complexion that is heightened by the pallor of porcelain, the shimmer of satin, the veneer of old furniture, and that an ordered regimen of exquisite nurture maintains at its best. Their necks moved easily in their low cravats, their long whiskers fell over their turned-down collars, they wiped their lips upon handkerchiefs with embroidered initials that gave forth a subtle perfume.[12]

Poets, too, have used dress as a topic for their readers to reflect upon. Their compressed form of presentation spurs the reader to respond, often emotionally, to imagery of an individual's dress. For example, Herrick wrote: "When as in silks my Julia goes, then, then, methinks how sweetly flows that liquefaction of her clothes." [13]

Biography is also part of literature. Descriptions of details of dress give historical accuracy to the portrayal of an individual. For example, Mary Barelli Gallagher documented for posterity the outfit Jacqueline Kennedy wore for the swearing-in ceremony on Inauguration Day in January 1961:

I saw Jackie when she was finally dressed. Her outfit was captivating—a fawn-colored wool cloth coat with a little sable stand-up collar and muff to match. Her pillbox . . . matched the color of her coat. To combat the snows, Jackie wore elegant dark high-heeled, fur-trimmed boots.[14]

Autobiographies provide not only accurate details concerning the writer's clothing and appearance but also the feelings which the individual had about his attire. A particularly vivid description and poignant example comes from Maya Angelou:

The dress I wore was lavendar taffeta, and each time I breathed it rustled, and now that I was sucking in air to breathe out shame it sounded like crepe paper on the back of hearses. As I'd watched Momma put ruffles on the hem and cute little tucks around the waist, I knew that once I put it on I'd look like a movie star. (It was silk and made up for that awful color.) I was going to look like one of the sweet little white girls who were everybody's dream of what was right with the world. . . . But Easter's early morning sun had shown the dress to be a plain ugly cut-down from a white woman's once-was-purple throwaway. It was old-lady-long too, but it didn't hide my skinny legs, which had been greased with Blue Seal Vaseline and powdered with Arkansas red clay. The age-faded color made my skin look dirty like mud, and everyone in church was looking at my skinny legs.[15]

summary

Dress may be viewed as a beautiful object or as an art form in itself. In addition, dress is intertwined with other art forms. In the performing arts, dress is usually termed *costume* and serves a variety of functions necessary to the success of a particular expression of the art form. A performer's costume communicates the basic facts of age, sex, occupation, and personality to his audience just as everyday dress of an individual communicates to those with whom he interacts. However, performers require special services from costume that are not necessary in everyday life. Thus stage dress must accommodate body movement and be sturdily constructed; in addition, special theatrical lighting effects on costume must be considered as well as the distance between the performer and audience. The performer must find psychological support for his role from his costume in order to give a successful performance. Some performing arts seem to require special costumes for the performers. Different types of musical and dance performances are associated with specific dress.

The plastic media of the visual arts and written description or commentary of the literary arts use dress to portray individual characteristics.

IV

DRESS and SOCIETY

10

DRESS AND TRADITIONAL SOCIETIES

Variation in dress from place to place and individual to individual raises questions as to what factors encourage certain forms of dress and discourage others. One way we can analyze variation is to consider the kinds of dress that are likely to occur in different types of societies. *Ideal types* have often been used to facilitate this kind of analysis. A society described as an ideal type does not exist anywhere in the world exactly as it is described; however, real societies can be understood as they are classified as more or less like one or another ideal type.

Four ideal types that allow classification of most known societies are: the folk society, the agrarian society, the urban-industrial society, and the mass society.[1] The folk society and the agrarian society are often referred to as traditional societies since they are governed by custom and sentiment. The urban-industrial and mass society, more simply referred to as industrial societies, are oriented to change and rational human relations.

In this chapter we will analyze traditional types of societies that may limit or encourage characteristics in dress. Dress in the non-industrial folk society will be discussed first, then some of the differences that would be expected in a settled agrarian society. Discussion of changes in dress that accompany industrialization and the transition from the urban-industrial state to mass society will be included in Chapter Eleven.

the folk society

The folk society as an ideal type has been elaborated by Redfield.[2] This is a preindustrialized society that is not known in the Western world today, although an approximation has been known in the past and is presently known in a few non-Western areas. The folk type of society includes a small number of people who have little or no communication with outside people. With little outside contact, they tend to inbreed and, therefore, to become biologically homogeneous: for example, in body form, and in hair and skin color. The family is the basic social unit that guides people's lives and most activities are within the family group. This type of society has no real law, history, or science since these activities depend on written records and no writing system exists. Because people in this small, isolated type of society come constantly into contact with the same limited physical environment and with the same small group of people, and because they perform similar tasks and take part in similar activities, they come to have very similar beliefs and outlooks on life.

Continual conditioning within the limited bounds of the small community gives each individual a strong sense of belonging to his society and makes conforming to custom simply a matter of habit. No one questions how things are done; everyone simply knows what is right behavior. Any deviation from customary behavior is resented, for tradition has, for the folk society, a sacred value and is not to be questioned. It serves as a guide for all problem solving and the elders are the decision makers. The older people are highly respected and looked up to since, by virtue of having lived the longest, they have accumulated the most experiences and, therefore, actually know the most.

Since the basic issue in life is biological survival, human activities focus on getting enough food and warding off threatening environmental forces. By hunting and gathering they obtain food and materials that may be converted, using hand power with primary tools, into clothing or shelter. Secondary and tertiary tools, that is those used to make other tools, are few. The people are self-sufficient since they produce what they consume and consume what they produce. Belief in supernatural forces permeates life. Sacred rituals and ceremonies aid in coping with the environment in the struggle for survival.

dress in the folk society

In the folk society we can expect the form of dress and adornment to be closely related to the simplicity of the technology. With few tools, only hand power, and no husbanding of plants and animals, people are limited to materials that they can find occurring naturally in their environment and that they can use without much processing. Naturally occurring materials, such as white clay mixed with water or ashes from the campfire, are types of materials that can be used for body decoration. Feathers can be used to decorate hair or can be shredded and stuck on the skin with animal blood. Shells that can be strung together on animal sinews or fibrous stems are easily available for body ornament along coastal areas. Materials that can be used as coverings with little processing include animal skins and hides, although simple weaponry and skinning tools are required. Leaves and grasses also can be tied together for simple cloaks or skirts.

With restrictions on materials and limited ability to produce, the folk society can provide only limited choice in kinds of dress. Dependence on traditional ways reinforces limitations on forms of dress, for innovation that breeds variety is discouraged and customary dress supported. If choices are few, people will tend to dress more or less alike which results in a similarity in appearance that strengthens the impression of group closeness and unity and encourages similarity in activity. The main variation is likely to be in distinctive dress for men and women; in most societies men and women do dress differently, even if the difference is no more than a tattoo, a nose ring, a necklace, or the way a piece of cloth is wrapped. These differences are probably symbolic of the difference between the tasks of males and females. Change in form of dress may occur, but it is likely to be so slow as to be almost indetectible.

Ultimately, respected position in the traditional society goes only to those who conform in dress—an individual is neither accepted nor recognized as a full member of the society unless he conforms. Dress thus distinguishes the faithful from the unfaithful, the insider from the outsider. Not only may dress be a symbol of general belonging to the society, it may also have specific symbolisms which indicate characteristics such as marital status, ceremonial status, mood, or prowess as a warrior. Whatever the symbolism, it will be clearly understood by the members of the folk society although it may not be so easily understood by outsiders. Where written symbolism is missing, nonverbal symbols such as dress take on increasing details in meaning; each bead in a necklace, each fold in a cloak may have a special meaning.

In the folk society younger people follow the directions of their elders in matters of dress. This transfer of accepted ways of doing things to the young helps insure that the order of the past is preserved in the present, in dress and other matters of behavior as well.

Religion is often the focal institution around which activities are organized, art the means of expressing the religion. What have separated out in the industrial society as the performing arts, the visual arts, and the practical arts associated with housing and dress are closely bound together among folk people; and singing, dancing, sculpture, painting, masks and costumes, utensils, basketry, ceramics, and architecture are likely to be complements to religious expression. White beads worn by a Zulu, for example, may be only decoration to the outsider, but to the Zulu they are necessary equipment for negotiations with supernatural beings:

A full-fledged isanusi *(Zulu diviner) covers himself with opaque white beads, some are worn on the head and they hang in veil-like fashion over the region of the eyes right around the head. Some beads are worn round the waist, arms, wrists, ankles and as sashes over both shoulders. These beads fortify the man against the apparitions that are said to speak through him. An* isanusi *gets his wisdom from the* emadloti *(spirits of ancestors). They speak through him. He is their agent, therefore, in their presence he must appear in white beads.*[3]

the agrarian society

Agrarian societies develop as people learn to use specific geographical areas for farming and herding. Such societies reach back as far as the civilizations of ancient Egypt, Mesopotamia, and the Indus River valley. These societies, neither so small nor so isolated as the folk type, had acquired the characteristics of a civilization:

A large enough population to have something resembling an urban agglomeration, a highly developed division of labor with concomitant specialization in a stratified society, food production rather than hunting and gathering, the form of government known as a "state," a calendar and basic mathematical knowledge, written records.[4]

Since in the agrarian society most people live in a simple settled farming or herding economy, wealth and position derive mainly from landholding although position in a priesthood or control over warriors armed to defend the community are other routes to power and prestige. A hereditary aristocracy comes to own the land which provides power and wealth; serving the aristocracy are agricultural workers and craftsmen who work in their homes. In such an economy surpluses develop and also a market for exchange of surplus goods. Specialization of labor evolves since surplus goods can be exchanged for goods that a person does not produce himself. The city can also develop since it depends on the production of surplus by agriculturists and craftsmen. The society, however, remains nonindustrial and production is mainly by hand power, supported by some animal power. And society is ordered by tradition and sentiment just as in the folk society. Feudal Europe was agrarian; in the twentieth century areas of Southeast Asia, Africa, and Latin America have continued to have large peasant (agrarian) groups lying outside the dominance of the urban industrial type of society developed in the major cities.

Primary contacts with family and neighbors are, as in the folk society, typical kinds of human relations, although the middle-man begins to emerge: the shopkeeper, the banker. There is cultural variety within limits, but custom and convention still direct life patterns and ritual reinforces custom. Literacy enhances the position of the thinking man, versus the man of strength and action. The hallowed position of the older man as the repository of knowledge is

(a)

(b)

Fig. 10–1. In the agrarian society, spinning and weaving are done by hand as in northern Okinawan villages. These photos show the villagers (a) tying banana fibers together to prepare them for spinning, (b) spinning banana fibers into yarn, (c) tying yarns to prepare them for dyeing, (d) using the tie-dyed

168

(c)

(d)

(e)

yarns in weaving banana cloth called *kasuri*, and (e) finishing the *kasuri* cloth by a smoothing or pressing process done by hand with a hot stone. (Courtesy of Lenore Landry.)

lessened. Libraries emerge. Art expands with technology and the lessening of the necessity for devoting most of one's time to survival. Art may be for art's sake only, not always tied to religion, body decoration, or utilitarian objects.

dress in the agrarian society

Type of dress is related to development of an agricultural and craft economy. With a settled population, fiber production and cultivation occurs. Different fibers have been used in different parts of the world, but wool and flax are two of the earliest known fibers to be converted into cloth: the ancient Egyptians were early users of flax, the ancient Sumerians of wool. Cotton spinning and weaving were developed in both ancient India and among the Inca. A textile technology requires the development, typically, of at least spinning

Fig. 10–2. A traditional Japanese kimono exhibits economy in the use of fabric.

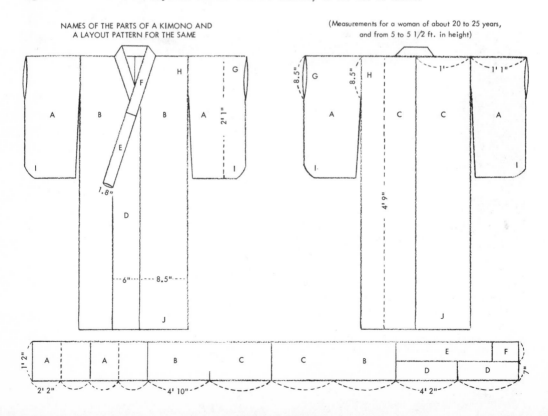

Fig. 10–3. In the class society, in which the peasant class have few economic resources, competition in dress thrives only among upper classes; great differences in dress exist between the rich and poor. (From *The Book of Hours* by the Duke de Berry. Courtesy of Peter Adelberg, Inc., European Art Color Slides Company.)

and weaving techniques, ordinarily organized in home crafts. Because woven fabrics take a long time to make by hand, counting the growing, harvesting, processing, spinning, and weaving time involved, there is a tendency to exert an economy in the use of fabrics. Societies with only a modestly developed craft may utilize forms of cloth as they come directly from the loom with little cutting or subdividing. The Egyptians, Greeks, and Romans all used clothes made of rectangles of cloth with little cutting. The Indian sari and the Japanese kimono both exhibit this kind of economy.

As differential wealth and position grow out of control of landholding within agrarian societies, sharp social class differences tend to grow, often distinguished by dress. Those who control landholding and members of the priesthood are likely to have the finest dress. For example, servants in Egypt were often nude while their masters and mistresses dressed in elaborate headdresses and jewelry and priests wore leopard skins. Body coverings, as contrasted with jewelry and accessory, were rather simple; but prestige could be shown by the numbers of layers worn. The latter practice was also characteristic of Greece where sumptuary laws were passed to limit the number of garments that might be worn at the same time.

In the class society in which the peasant class has few economic resources, competition in dress thrives only among upper classes since only the wealthy can afford the costumes that utilize scarce resources and take much time to make. Change in form of dress, then, is typical of the upper classes; little change can be seen in the dress of the poor which differs greatly from that of the rich. Dress is thus a powerful symbol of status distinguishing between classes and categories within classes. Sumptuary law may support these distinctions. Status is generally fixed by birth and an individual has little chance of acquiring the symbols of status of a group he is not born into.

summary

Dress in traditional societies is largely determined by custom and tradition. In the folk society variation may occur as items of dress are individually handcrafted and precise copying of designs is not an achievable goal. However, variety is generally discouraged by a limited technology and the scarcity of materials that can be directly converted into costume without much processing. Items of dress may acquire intricate symbolic significance, often magical or religious, since forms of dress are stable and time allows them to acquire meanings that can be readily learned by everyone.

Change in form of dress is more prevalent in the agrarian society with development of textile crafts that encourage cultivation of fibers that can be converted into cloth. Much variety in clothing, however, is a privilege of a wealthy upper class that can afford to own a number of costumes, or discard old costumes in favor of something new.

11

DRESS AND
INDUSTRIAL
SOCIETIES

urban-industrial society

The urban-industrial society is far removed in character from the traditional folk and agrarian societies and is transitional to the mass society. It is based on an organization of people far different from the family organization of the folk society, or the class system of the agrarian society. The industrial process itself is:

. . . *a means of production combining technology, centralized production, and the specialization of labor. Thus industrialism means a well-developed productive technology, removal of the productive process from the home to the factory, the substitution of routinized and specialized job tasks for crafts and skilled workmanship, the standardization of work procedures and products, and the centralization of decision and management functions.*[1]

In the urban-industrial society large numbers of people live in densely settled areas so as to have accesss to the unit of production, distribution, or governmental administration with which they are associated in some kind of occupational relationship. The occupational structure is complex with people highly dependent upon each other for production of goods and services desired. Exchange of goods may be through great distance; hence society-wide markets and marketing systems arise. Great cultural and occupational variety is a product of evolutionary changes promoted by a highly developed technology. Industry of high productive capacity requires workers of many different skills in order to provide a great variety of goods and services. Efficient means of transportation and communication distribute these goods and services, and information on them, society-wide, and, furthermore add to variety by facilitating cross-cultural exchange.

Stratification is complex, related to an equally complex division of labor: managerial classes, white collar workers, laborers, a moneyed elite, and numerous intermediary groups are characteristic.

The bureaucracy is the typical method of organizing personnel for efficient production, providing routinized ways for arriving at decisions and for defining tasks and responsibilities. A hierarchy of authority becomes clearly understood, and rational decisions not based on emotions or sentiments are expected. The corporation is the typical way of organizing the management of business and industry and depends on a large-scale bureaucracy.

Since conflicts cannot be resolved by simple application of social pressure, various interest groups, such as consumers and minority groups, organize specialized agencies to influence decision-making. In general, laws, instead of the sentiments and sanctions of kin and neighbors, govern behavior.

The society is heterogeneous, that is individuals vary widely in their personal characteristics, including their knowledge, beliefs, and values. It is typically biologically heterogeneous as a result of much crossbreeding of different biological types from widely scattered segments of a large population. People gain different knowledge and develop differences in values and beliefs as they have varied life experiences, and are in contact with large numbers of people in many life settings. In addition, individuals perform a variety of roles, including those at work, at home, and in the community. But since all do not perform the same roles, social diversity is increased.

Although people come in contact with many other people, most contact is impersonal and secondary contacts ordinarily exceed primary ones. Contact with others may also be only indirect, that is through mass media. As close social contact with other people is made more difficult to achieve by the impersonal nature of the city, feelings of anonymity and alienation may be generated.

Much value is placed on change and great faith is placed on the ability of people to find ways of effecting desired changes particularly through the application of science. Tradition is, therefore, de-emphasized as a means for guiding behavior. Economic gain becomes an important motive for behavior as individuals' lives are less circumscribed by traditions of family and religion. Nevertheless, they are placed in economic interdependence and cannot survive without each other. Since mass produced items are available to large proportions of the population, tendencies toward a homogeneous life-style as represented by material possessions develop. In contrast to what happens in traditional societies, the young develop prestige, for they have access to knowledge through a variety of mass media and can challenge the knowledge of their elders.

dress in urban-industrial society

Dress in urban-industrial society can be analyzed in relation to machine manufacture, role shifts, the acceleration in fashion change, dependence on dress symbols, and problems of choice among multiple alternatives. Each of these factors influences the dress of individuals in the society.

Machine Manufacture

Dress in urban-industrial society, for example the U.S. from about 1860 to 1940, shows characteristics that are related to a conversion from hand to machine production. Textile manufacture was converted to machines more quickly than garment manufacture. In garment manufacture, the sewing machine was a key invention in speeding the production of garments. Later simplification and standardization of form of dress occurred as mass production methods made rapid manufacture of multiple copies of the same model possible.

Fig. 11–1. In the industrial society, spinning, weaving, and finishing are done largely by machine. (a) Fibers are straightened and pulled into a strand of fibers by machine as a preliminary step for spinning; (b) spinning yarn in the industrial society is a mechanized process; (c) package dyeing shown on p. 177 is a method used for dyeing yarns; (d) weaving in the industrialized society is typically performed in large "loom rooms" by automation; (e) an example of one of the most complex machines for weaving is the jacquard loom; and (f) one of the final phases on the automated finishing line is a smoothing or pressing process done by heated rollers. (Courtesy of American Textile Manufacturers Institute.)

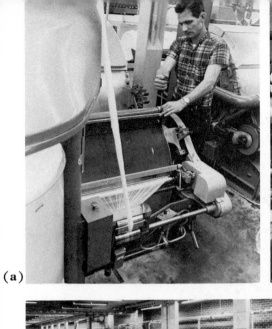

(a)

(b)

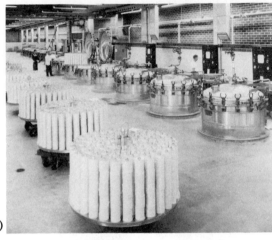

(c)

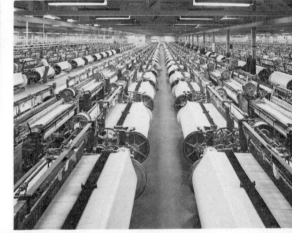

(d)

(e)

(f)

Fig. 11–2. Machines are used to cut layers of garment pieces and the process of cutting is speeded up from hand production cutting. (Courtesy of the American Apparel Manufacturers Association.)

Fig. 11–3. In the urban-industrial society, multiple copies of the same model are made possible by a system of mass production. (Courtesy of the American Apparel Manufacturers Association.)

In societies that are in transition from agrarian to industrial most apparel production is accomplished by combining machine and hand techniques. Even in rather highly industrialized societies some garment production techniques are likely to be executed by hand.

Competition in the market place also contributes to simplification in styles. Since the garment may sell best that costs a few cents less, costs may be reduced by simplifying design so that the necessary operations for construction of a garment are fewer in number. Producing from the same pattern season after season also reduces costs. Thus a man's shirt made by machine becomes standardized in form and requires far less time for its production than a handmade one. Variety is developed through fabric color and texture rather than cut of garment.

In most industrializing societies, men's clothing has become standardized more quickly and more completely than women's. By the 1890s most kinds of American men's apparel were made in factories by machine; not until 1920 was the same true for much of women's apparel. This type of difference has probably occurred as men have had different relationships to the activities spawned by the industrial society than have women.

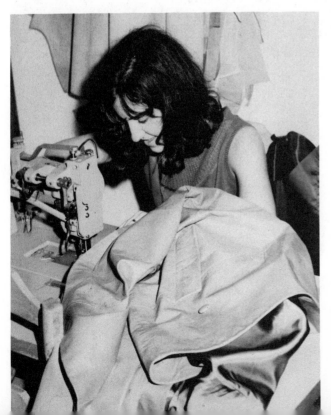

Fig. 11–4. Hand and machine processes are used for making leather garments in Spain. (Courtesy of Lenore Landry.)

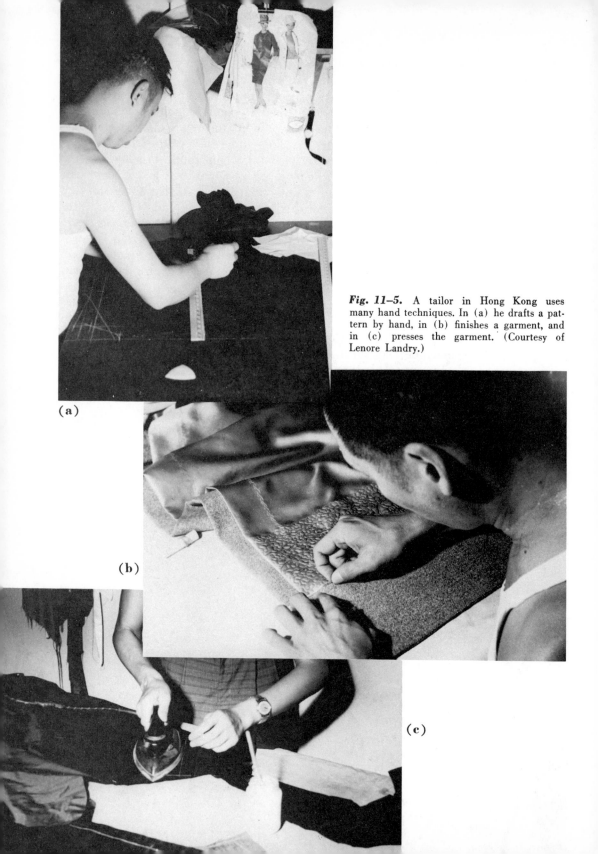

(a)

(b)

(c)

Fig. 11–5. A tailor in Hong Kong uses many hand techniques. In (a) he drafts a pattern by hand, in (b) finishes a garment, and in (c) presses the garment. (Courtesy of Lenore Landry.)

Changing Roles

Change from hand to machine labor alters the ways in which people work and live together, and dress reflects this change. Clothes required for work in a factory may be different from those worn for work on a farm. In addition, being thrown into daily contact with fellow workers may require "a minimum decency" of a worker if he is to fit in and work harmoniously with others. Thus in the families of industrial wage earners in America between 1890 and World War I, clothing expenditures had to adjust so the man of the family could be properly clothed. On the average, he spent a third more than his wife for clothing.[2] A somewhat similar relation in family expenditures occurred among a majority of Nigerian cocoa farmers' families in the 1950s.[3]

As men move into work outside the home, women tend, at least at first, to remain in the home where they are responsible for providing for food and clothing needs, tending children, and taking care of the house. In the United States, nineteenth-century industrialization brought sharp distinction between men's and women's dress. Although women were strongly tied to household tasks, their husbands' work outside the home brought increased prosperity, and more women in middle social levels had the money to buy fashionable dress.

As industrialization has spread throughout the world, Western-type dress has also spread, frequently because of attached prestige as well as standardized production. In other countries, as in America, women have tended to lag behind in adopting factory-produced clothes. Some groups in which the men have abandoned the traditional and adopted Western dress more quickly than women are: the Highland Indians of the Andes of Ecuador, Peru, and Bolivia; the Yorubas of Nigeria; the Japanese; and the Hindus of India.

Generally in an industrial society wide choice in kinds of dress exists although there is not completely free choice. That is, not all conceivable choices are acceptable. Wide choice depends on and reflects volume production and relatively free role choice. American people, for example, have some choice in the role they wish to play at a particular time. Individuals may dress for occasion or for mood using different types of clothing: lounging clothes, office clothes, school clothes, and different types of hair styles and cosmetics.

People are not molded to just one consistent type in appearance

Fig. 11–6. In the United States, nineteenth-century industrialization brought sharp distinctions between men's and women's dress. Contrasts are shown in their 1870s dress.

and dress. Instead, with different backgrounds and experience they are likely to come to different decisions concerning dress. However, as they develop different patterns of dress, complete anarchy is not the result—some consistency and typing, often on a local basis, occurs. Dress in one city may be subtly different from that in another: New York City may offer more range in costume than Madison, Wisconsin, or Ames, Iowa. Variety also results as there are many roles that people may fulfill beyond doing a man's work or a woman's work as in folk or agrarian societies. Roles are associated with assembly line workers, office workers, salesmen, managers, construction workers, foremen, teachers, students, doctors, and lawyers, and appropriate costume can be defined for each role.

Although unique costume may not always be developed for each role, certain phrases show that some types of dress become very closely associated with certain roles: "White collar," "blue collar," "women in white," "battle fatigues." Words like hippy, beatnik, mod, and rocker in recent times and beau, dandy, and dude in by-gone days evoke mental pictures of appearance associated with roles.

Acceleration in Fashion Change

Rapid change is characteristic of dress in the industrial society, just as it is characteristic of most aspects of industrial life. Spinning machines, power looms, and sewing machines are only a few of the types of machines that speed up the conversion of raw materials into items of dress. All the industrial apparatus of the textile and clothing industries feed goods into markets where it is distributed to consumers. In the United States, a complex fashion system involving an intricate relationship among consumers and both foreign and domestic producers and distributors facilitates rapid change in dress. But all parts of this fashion system must be prepared for change, and the speed of change must be carefully calculated, if change is to occur. Resistance to change in dress was shown in 1970 by women who picketed against the *midi* and seemed unprepared for as drastic a change as producers and distributors were proposing in dress lengths.

Dependence on Dress Symbols

Another characteristic of dress in industrial society is dependence on clothing cues (the language of dress) in social encounters. Few people, of the many contacted daily, are known intimately. There-fore, reactions to others depend a great deal upon appraisals of the cues that dress provides. People react to those they do not know according to how they interpret their appearance.

However, the symbolism of dress is not greatly elaborated; that is, specific meanings are not attributed to every fine detail of a costume. Intricacies of meaning do not develop, as for traditional costume, since the *ever-changing* costume, possible in a mass society, usually does not have time enough to earn a complicated traditional symbolism. Uniforms and badges that carry instant messages can come and go.

Deception is also possible, for people have the freedom to "create their own types of selves" to some extent with the wide variety of clothes and cosmetics available to all social levels. One of the

Fig. 11–7. The naval uniform and the monk's habit were part of the credentials Fred Demara used to pass himself off as a naval surgeon and Trappist Monk. (Courtesy of (a) James F. Coyne, (b) *Time,* © 1959, and (c) Studio Roger Bedard, Montreal.

classic examples of an elaborate hoax concerning identity was perpetuated by Fred Demara who never finished high school yet was able to pass himself off as naval surgeon, psychology professor, cancer researcher, dean of a school of philosophy, Latin teacher, deputy warden of a state penitentiary, and Trappist monk. The naval uniform, monk's habit, surgeon's gown were part of the credentials he presented to make his deception successful.[4]

Problems of Choice among Multiple Alternatives

The urban society allows alternatives in choices for dress. Rights and wrongs in dress are neither so rigidly or explicitly defined, nor so pervasive, as in a traditional society. Permissiveness exists because there is no one tradition. Intead, there are multiple traditions for dress, extending locally more often than society wide. Moreover, conflicting standards for dress co-exist. As Americans, for example, move from one social orbit to another, they often have to learn new patterns for dress or else suffer social discomfort. Not the sharp reprimand or punishment characteristic of traditional societies but the subtle rebuke, disdainful stare, or unextended invitation encourages conforming. In general, the meanings of dress must be looked for in local contexts; what looks like permissiveness in dress, society wide, does not rule out fairly rigid standards within local groups and subgroups. Permissiveness in America is indicated by a lack of extensive, nationwide standards. Most of the time the wearing of clothing is required and there is a fairly consistent refusal to allow men to wear clothes defined as women's. Laws support these standards. Otherwise, local variation is the pattern.

The young person in modern urban society wields more influence than the old in setting patterns of dress. A major ideal of beauty or handsomeness is youth, in a world in which a large percent of the population is 25 years and under and in a literate world which enables the young to compete for status with older people.

mass society

Industrialism, urbanism, bureaucracy, and mass media are transforming the urban industrial society into what many call the mass society. Concentrations of large numbers of people in large metropolitan areas result in the city, particularly as it is seen in America, being the nucleus of *mass* activity. It is the setting for mass production of goods, mass marketing, and mass consumption. Major educational, religious, and political, as well as financial institutions are also found in the city. In addition it is the seat of communications systems that penetrate every part of the society. As a result of the efficiency of these systems, residents of rural areas and small towns have access to mass culture largely emanating from large cities.

Probably most outstanding in the mass society is (1) the efficiency of productive units in providing a tremendous volume of output and (2) the overwhelming influence of mass media. According to Martindale, in 1850 in America only 35 percent of work output was by machine while in 1950, 99 percent was by machine.[5] Automated technology adds to the efficiency of production at many levels of activity and the computer replaces and supplements mental power of humans as other machines replace and supplement physical activities. Mass communication reflects this efficiency in the widespread influence of its media: radio, movies, and television as well as newspapers and magazines. These media encourage consensus in choice among mass-produced products and thereby act as organizing mechanisms within mass society. They familiarize people with competing products, show consumption trends, and reflect values and ideologies of American society.

Also characteristic of the mass society are very large bureaucratic structures in government as well as business and industry. As these large structures spread their influence nationwide, they reduce the autonomy of local communities.

In business the corporate form of ownership dominates and ownership is distributed throughout society through stockholders and boards of directors. Small businessmen and farmers are reduced in number and those in the white collar classes increased. Education and achievement become a means to status within the bureaucratic structure of the society, and hereditary expectations for position are deemphasized.

dress in mass society

In the mass society, science and technology have reduced risk in the production of materials utilized in dress, by replacing naturally occurring materials with man-made. Thus many kinds of garments and accessories can be made of synthetic materials, whose production is not dependent on the vagaries of weather. These materials may be converted into fiber or fabric, or molded directly into useful or ornamental shapes. Figures in Table 1 show the upward trend in world production of man-made fibers since 1950.

TABLE 1.   **World production of man-made and major natural fibers.***

	1950 %	1960 %	1970 %
Man-made fibers	18	22	39
Raw cotton	71	68	53
Raw wool	11	10	8

* *Textile Organon*, XXXIV, No. 6 (June, 1963), 79; and XLII, No. 6 (June, 1971), 74.

Fig. 11–8. In the mass society more hand operations are necessary in apparel manu-facture than in the manufacture of textiles, although mass production methods speed up production of garments. (Courtesy of the American Apparel Manufacturers Associa-tion.)

Development of synthetic fibers adds to the variety of character-istics that apparel can have. A number of generic types of synthetic fibers have been developed and within any generic type, wide dif-ferences in characteristics are possible since modifications can be made at many different stages of their production. However, greater variety in characteristics of natural fiber products is also being made possible by chemical and physical modification of the natural fibers.

More hand operations are still necessary in apparel manufacture than in the manufacture of textiles, although many processes are now being automated, or on the verge of being automated. The *Journal of the Apparel Research Foundation* regularly reports in-novations in apparel sewing and assembling. Machines are engi-neered for many specific, automatic, or semiautomatic operations: to fold and attach shirt pockets, to "uncurl" knit fabrics during sewing, to sew on labels, to hem a shirt front and pass it on to a

Fig. 11–9. Computerized pattern making is an example of advanced technology in mass society. (Courtesy of the American Apparel Manufacturers Association.)

button sewing machine, to thread needles, to stitch contour seams, to stitch the left front fly of men's trousers and slacks, to fold shorts or T-shirts.[6]

Computerized pattern grading services are offered to manufacturers by companies that file with a computer information from one typical manual graded pattern for knit and woven apparel items, such as cut and sewn dresses, shirts, and sportswear.[7] Graded patterns then are turned out on order.

Perhaps one of the greatest breaks with prehistoric technology will occur if the search for "stitchless" seaming is successful. Late Stone Age man conceived the principle of the eyed needle, and so far no one has replaced his invention as a means for assembling fabric pieces into three-dimensional shapes for dress. Some molding of boots, hats, and helmets is done, otherwise most enclosing garments and accessories of human beings are sewn. Ultrasonically sealed seams are proposed as one alternate to sewing.

Some methods use adhesives, while others depend on a natural molecular bond between the plies of fabrics without adding other materials. Some use heat, some use pressure, some use both heat and pressure. Some require only contact. Some are limited to pure thermoplastic fibers and will not work on thermoset or natural fibers.[8]

(Thermoplastic fibers are those that can be softened or melted by heat, while thermoset fibers cannot be resoftened or melted.)

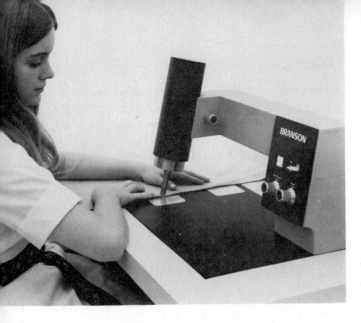

Fig. 11–10. Ultrasonically sealed seams are proposed as one alternative to sewing. (Courtesy of the American Apparel Manufacturers Association.)

Fig. 11–11. The cutting of fabric without scissors or knives but by computer-controlled laser fabric cutter is a recent and revolutionary breakthrough in apparel manufacture. (Courtesy of the American Apparel Manufacturers Association.)

Perhaps as revolutionary a concept as nonstitched seams is the cutting of fabric without scissors or knives—as has been done by a computer-controlled laser fabric-cutting machine demonstrated in 1971.[9]

If automation can help turn out mass products more and more efficiently, rapid communication and transport can bring fad and fashion quickly to all regions of society. Anyone can obtain the mass style-of-life symbols that fashion provides. On one hand, great conformity in a large area is possible, depending on the controls exerted, such as governmental or ideological. On the other hand, great variety is possible, simply because of the efficiency of an industrial system that can put out many alternate forms in a competitive market.

An individual's choice of dress reflects two general orientations to the large organizational structures and heterogeneity characteristic of mass society: accommodation and reaction.

Accommodation

Accommodation implies an acceptance of a work ethic such as has been generated by promises of rewards within the industrial system. It may occur as a result of emphasis on interpersonal relations in the network of white collar jobs: dress may be carefully manipulated in order to control interaction with others—to keep one's self acceptable, "salable," and influential within the big corporation. The image of efficiency projected by a sober, dark suit, "discrete" color contrast in shirt and tie, and meticulous grooming epitomizes the corporate man with self subordinated to the tasks demanded.

Another kind of accommodation can be seen in a tendency for shared style-of-life symbols, such as dress, rather than shared beliefs or ideology to be a basis for drawing people together. Boorstein refers to this sharing as he speaks of the evolving of a "consumption community."[10] According to him, entrance to the community is democratic since one only needs enough money to provide himself with the material goods common to the life-style. Clothing, home, household furnishings, and automobile mark affiliation with the community and distinguish insiders from outsiders. Deprivation consists of not having the ability to consume like others. A feeling of shared well-being, shared risks, common interests, and common concerns comes to people from consuming the same kinds of objects.

Reaction

Some of the reactions to mass society shown in dress are suggested by Klapp.[11] We shall examine three of these: dandyism, ego-screaming, and puritanism.

DANDYISM
This is a kind of rejection of an ethic of hard work. Dandies live for display rather than devotion to work. Participation in the life of the dandy, in other centuries a privilege of a wealthy elite, becomes democratized in the mass society as those who have the money can participate.

EGO-SCREAMING
The individual who uses dress for ego-screaming utilizes shock value in his dress to set himself apart and thus to establish that he exists as an individual in the eyes of others as well as himself. His behavior may represent a reaction to the impersonal nature of urbanized society that connects people on a rational, functional basis only, or may be a reaction to a loss of individual influence within the large social structures of mass society.

PURITANISM
The puritan in dress sets himself above "ordinary" people who submit to social demands. He is modest in his apparel, and abstains from great interest in appearance, which he may define in various ways: as being materialistic, hedonistic, square, conformist. His act may be a rejection of the work ethic that has as a goal the acquiring of money that may be used for buying consumer goods—he consumes only minimally.

Developments within mass society may have some effect on cultural preferences for appearances and traditional symbolism for certain social roles. In the transition from work based on physical strength to that based on mental abilities, status differences among those of different physical characteristics are reduced. Nevertheless, traditional biases may exist such as a cultural preference for large men and small women and dress which emphasizes these traditional preferences.

Although in industrializing society distinctions between men's and women's dress may be accentuated, distinctions may be somewhat reduced in mass society as individuals look for their identity elsewhere. Often stronger distinctions on the basis of age appear than on the basis of sex.

the art of dress
in mass society

In the industrialized and mass societies art has a less pervasive influence in matters of daily human concern than in traditional societies. Nevertheless artistic endeavors are still interwoven with aspects of people's lives. Most people demonstrate some interest in beauty, whether in nature, people, identified works of art, or objects of everyday use like dress. Unlike in folk and agrarian societies where utility and art blend, the artist in the industrial society may specialize in creating things that he considers beautiful with no concern for their usefulness. In fact, two categories of creators of the visual arts are distinguished on the basis of whether or not they have an intent to create something useful. Titles such as industrial designer, architect, landscape architect, dress designer, interior designer, and commercial artist separate out those who have concern for creating something that is simultaneously useful and beautiful. The painter, the sculptor, the print maker are committed only to the latter, that is, creating the beautiful. In addition, participation in the artistic experience becomes compartmentalized—the "consuming" role becomes separated distinctly from the "producing" role, and many individuals participate in art more as spectators than as creators. Or, as in the case of dress, an individual wearer becomes largely an organizer of items of dress produced by someone else.

Although art in traditional and industrial society appears to be different, Linton's opinion is that, in spite of religion's being a strong inspiration for art expression in the folk society, the motives of the folk artist and his industrial counterpart are much the same. He believes that each works because of an inner desire to reach beauty, profit, or prestige, or some combination thereof; each may also work simply because aesthetic activities are expected of a person in his position.[12] Wingert also points out that religious concerns do not always completely subordinate other considerations in creation of art in folk societies. He notes the irrepressible nature of the aesthetic impulse, and the importance of personal prestige, as strong forces motivating their art.[13] Thus objects made for personal adornment may indeed provide aesthetic pleasure, but they may also signify individual achievement, such as initiation into a religious society, and thereby enhance personal status as well as identify religious connections.

Some differences in approach to aesthetics of dress in the folk and the industrial society become apparent as we consider how the individual in the latter society learns to verbalize and rationalize an aesthetic philosophy. The individual in folk society does not intellectualize his art; he approaches it as something that is felt rather than talked about. In industrial society the aesthetic aspects of dress are both "talked about" and felt.

As we consider the art of dress in mass society, we realize an individual may act as executor of designs, arranger, displayer, or spectator confronted with the effect of his own or others' arrangements of dress. Although the displayer role is available to all, and certainly most people retain some control over the arranging role, other roles indicated can be shared, especially as a society industrializes and develops specialists to perform specific tasks. The photographer's model is a fairly unique example of someone who turns over arrangement of his or her appearance to someone else—at least during working hours. When the model is not before the camera, he resumes control of his personal display. On the other hand, persons who fashion accessory and apparel with their own hands according to their own designs, and for their own use, are participating the most fully in the art of dress.

As many items of dress are produced in the factory, and an array of technicians aid in the process of body ornament and covering, an individual's direct role in producing the items he will use to arrange his appearance is reduced; however, the complexity of his arranging role may be increased. He must depend on the varied output of many specialized producers: shoemakers, jewelry makers, garment makers, wig makers, beauty appliance makers, hair stylists, beauticians, cosmetic and other manufacturers, and his dependence may be world-wide, not just community-wide. His choice making is complicated for he must choose from a wide variety of products and services.

Coverings and body ornamentation for the very wealthy may be designed by specialists, whether jewelers, weavers, dress designers, hair dressers, or barbers. In one sense, the creative experience is thereby removed from the wearer. However, the individual adds to his costume his own gestures, stance, and carriage and at least a minimum of his own arranging or disarranging. Depending on the individual to whom services are given, the specialist may be indeed imposing his art; on the other hand, he may simply be exercising his skills to create the model which the client desires but does not have the skills or dexterity to execute. Cutting one's own hair, for instance, has built-in obstacles to successful execution, even if one has mastered the skill of cutting the hair of others.

social consensus and dress

As we examine dress within any society, we must remember that probably *no* society is purely traditional, or purely industrial, as described. Instead each society exhibits its own unique blend of what is traditional and what is not.

In the traditionally oriented, nonliterate folk societies, classifications of the beautiful and nonbeautiful in appearance become part of customary belief and are largely accepted without question. Within large, industrial societies, characterized by a propensity for change, the power of custom is less strong and acceptance of a standard for beauty is not nearly so automatic. Yet consensus is still a goal as a means of achieving order, evolving from shared beliefs as well as mutual human dependencies. Dependencies develop as people look to each other for assistance in taking care of their needs. A child requires someone to feed and protect him; his parents desire someone to carry on their blood line. A sick person wants someone to cure his ailments; a doctor must have someone to treat in order to practice his profession. The shoe salesman, and each of the individuals who help make, transport, and advertise a pair of shoes, need a customer to buy shoes as much as the customer needs all the people who help provide him with shoes. All are dependent on each other.

The arrival at something approaching consensus in the large, industrial society is an intricate social maneuver, for many alternative belief systems are likely to coexist and compete with each other. Moreover, the possibility for consensus in beliefs concerning something like dress and beauty in personal appearance is complicated by the great variety of products related to dress that can be produced in a highly industrialized society, and the capacity to institute rapid change in type of items produced.

In one way, the manner of arriving at consensus in beliefs concerning ideal appearance in different types of societies is very similar. Just as the nonliterate's concept of preferred appearance grows out of his immersion within his own culture, so does that of the individual in

Fig. 11–12. The popularity of the Beatles in the 1960s helped expose the public to a change in length of men's hair. (Courtesy of Culver Pictures, Inc.)

the large, literate society. However, each absorbs his culture differently. The nonliterate learns a way of life almost entirely through close person-to-person contact with a rather small number of people who share the same customs and beliefs. From them, because of their shared beliefs, he readily learns an attitude toward appearance consistent with an already existing consensus. In an industrialized society, like that in the United States, the individual also learns through contact with others; but he is, in addition, also bombarded by the visual and verbal cues of mass communication systems. By virtue of their ability to create simultaneous conditioning of large numbers of people by identical stimuli, these systems greatly encourage consensus on a large scale.

When communication via mass media is both pervasive and persuasive, initiating change and restating of consensus can be both rapid and widespread. If we consider the matter of dress, we can readily see how ways of dress may be suggested and promoted as the general public is exposed to certain kinds of dress more than others, and as some kinds of dress are presented in a more favorable light than others. The extensive coverage of the activities of the Beatles' musical group in newspapers, magazines, and television at the height of their popularity in the 1960s helped expose the public to a change in length of men's hair. Imitation was limited to a small number of the young at first. Gradually, however, more and more well-known figures of different ages and social background began to be seen, in person and via mass media, with longer hair. Thus sanctioned by a cross section of public figures of prestige, a male image that included longer hair became widely accepted, and a new consensus on attractiveness in hair length emerged.

summary

The form of dress in industrial societies is affected by the limits that machine production places on the manufacture of actual items of dress as well as the materials, such as textiles, from which they are made. Designs are simplified and multiple copies of designs are possible in machine manufacture.

However, increased volume resulting from the efficiency of machine production in the mass society expands the number of alternatives from which people can choose and hence allows considerable variety for any one person. However, ordering of choices throughout mass society occurs as the various communication media bombard large numbers of people with the same types of dress as visual stimuli. Consensus occurs as people become used to and accept those forms of dress most widely or favorably publicized.

12

Ann Corns Slocum

ECONOMIC DIMENSIONS OF DRESS

To understand the dress of the people in any society, we must also understand the economic factors within that society which affect an individual's choice of dress. Throughout most of this book *dress* has been used as the primary term to designate the subject of emphasis. However, when assessing dress and economic systems of societies, we find that most of the data available usually fall within the more specific categories of clothing or textile products. Therefore, in this chapter, many references are made to clothing, apparel, or textiles rather than to dress.

A cross-cultural view reveals economic similarities from society to society. In the first place, all societies are confronted by the problems of scarce resources and unlimited human wants. Secondly, they all have developed some kind of economic system to allocate scarce resources in relation to human wants.

scarce resources and
unlimited human wants

All people have a similar economic problem: resources are scarce relative to wants. As individuals, each of us can probably recall wanting some product, a new garment or a new stereo, for example, that we could not acquire because our resources, that is, our money, would not cover the purchase, or our time and skill would not allow us to make it. Cross-culturally, economics at a national level involves much the same problem: only limited natural resources are available, in relation to those needed, for production of all the goods and services that are needed or wanted by an increasing population.[1] A country has finite land areas suitable for agriculture, and for yielding gas or oil. Water, too, is limited. As a result, a search is almost always underway in all nations for ways to extend the use of limited natural resources. Within limitations, nature's yield may be augmented by application of technology, more efficient utilization of human energy and skill, and by obtaining products through trade with other nations. However, Heilbroner points out that where nature's yield has been increased in such ways, namely within industrial societies, human wants have increased correspondingly. Thus scarcity is caused not only by limitations in the physical environment, but also by rising human expectations,[2] for seldom, if ever, are there enough resources to satisfy the total needs and desires of a nation.

Providing for human wants requires the use of scarce resources. Economists use the term "economic good" to refer to those products made from scarce resources, and they define a resource as scarce when ". . . there is less available than people would like to consume if they could have it free."[3] Only if there is enough to satisfy everyone's wants at no cost, as is the case with air and sunshine, is a good considered "free." When considering the use of scarce resources, individuals usually think of the consumption of human energy and skill and material goods such as equipment or money. They are less aware that the goods that they purchase represent the usage of natural resources. Clothing, for example, represents the use of land, water, forest and petroleum products, and electrical energy. The importance of natural resources in clothing production can be illustrated by the use of one resource, land, for the production of cotton fiber. Between 1963-1968 in the United States an average of 4,292 million pounds of cotton fiber were used annually for domestic consumption or for export, and an average of 42.23 percent of this fiber, or 1,813 million pounds annually, went into the apparel end use. Of the fiber available 5.20 percent or about 94 million pounds came from imports; and an additional average of 120 million raw fiber equivalent pounds annually were imported as apparel. Dividing pounds consumed by the yield per acre, reveals that cotton apparel consumed in the United States represented an average annual use of 3,452,000 domestic acres and 495,000 foreign acres.[4]

existence of an economic system

Each nation has an economic system that provides a means of making decisions about the allocation of scarce resources and the organization of a system for production and distribution of goods for consumption. These decisions must be made because resources are limited, but always required, in the production of goods, and because wants are ever present and rising. An individual may use his available dollars to purchase a new coat, pay tuition, or make payments on a car. When purchasing a coat, for example, he may decide between a high fashion or a classic design. People rank priorities; and their values and goals provide the bases for ranking. Similarly, nations are faced with the question of what, and how much, will be produced: in consumer goods, military hardware, or industrial equipment. If consumer goods are high in priority, further decisions must be made as to what will be produced: appliances, automobiles, or clothing? The question of "how" goods will be produced must also be answered: decisions must be made concerning utilization of machinery versus human labor, the participants in the work force, and the tasks they will perform. A further question is: who will receive the goods that are produced? And, on what basis is income distributed? The mechanism used by a nation to answer these questions is called an economic system. Gordon suggests that the principles that guide the decisions stem from cultural values; thus the economic system should be viewed as a part of the total culture.[5]

factors affecting
clothing production and distribution

Providing for fiber and apparel wants of its people depends upon the quantity and variety of resources a society has available, its population/resource ratio, and its specific economic system that functions in decision-making about production and distribution.

Quantity and Variety of Resources

The fact that the resources that countries have at their command vary greatly in quantity as well as in variety or mix of specific resources creates national differences in patterns of clothing production. The composition of the resource mix includes such variables as climatic conditions, which includes seasonal and total precipitation, temperature and length of growing season, topography, water supply, and mineral deposits. In general, resources are more likely to be larger and the variety of resources greater as physical area of a country increases. Resource distribution, as it relates to textiles, is illustrated by the fact that India, Mexico, Egypt, and southern portions of the U.S. and U.S.S.R. are physically endowed to produce cotton that requires a temperate zone and thrives best with a fertile soil, high temperatures, abundant rainfall, and a great deal of sunshine. By contrast, portions of eastern Europe and northwestern European Russia, which are unsuitable for cotton production, are well suited to produce flax, which requires a medium loam or clay soil and a damp climate with heavy summer showers. Semi-arid areas in Australia, South Africa, Argentina, western United States, and Soviet Russia are unsuitable for cultivation, but can be grazed by sheep since they are capable of climbing over rough pastures, getting along with little water, and eating scanty foliage.[6]

Population/Resource Ratio

A second factor affecting production of clothing is the population/resource ratio, which can be defined as the ". . . relationship between the size and technical adequacy of a population on the one

200

hand and the quantity and quality of terrestrial resources on the other. . . ." [7] The significance of size of population was alluded to earlier in the observation that population growth demands more resources. Indonesia at the present time is a striking example of a country faced with resource problems created by population growth. With a growth rate of 2.9 percent the population will double in 24 years. Much of the increasing output of food, clothing, and other goods will then be utilized by the three million people added to the population each year. Thus little, if any, increased production will be left to raise living standards. [8]

Another example of the relationship of population size to other resources can be seen in the production of wool fiber. Sheep require space for grazing; and the predominance of wool production in the southern hemisphere is made possible, in part, by the stage of settlement, that is, the human population density is sufficiently low to allow room for what the economists refer to as an extensive animal industry. [9]

Up to this point resources have been discussed largely in terms of natural resources. The human population, however, is also a resource. For example, the textile industry is one of the first industries to be expanded by developing nations, in part because it can utilize hand production methods and employ large numbers of people. [10] The workers, who may be skilled in hand production methods, probably have little or no knowledge or skill in the operation of machinery for mass production. But a developing nation may capitalize on the size and/or skill level of its human resource to compensate for a lack of capital which would be needed to purchase equipment for mass production.

Alternative Economic Systems

A third factor affecting clothing production is the type of economic system that a country has. Very broadly one may categorize economic systems under the headings of *traditional, command or centrally planned,* and *market,* although in fact systems are mixed to some degree rather than being pure types.

Heilbroner describes a traditional system as a hereditary allocation of tasks. One's role in life is largely ascribed at birth, skills are passed on from generation to generation, and tradition, backed by sanctions of custom and law, provides a static solution to the questions of production and distribution. Reliance on tradition as an organizer of roles usually occurs in primitive agrarian or nonindustrial societies.[11] Reynolds uses the term "subsistence economy" to describe the family, clan, or tribe that produces ". . . all of its requirements and consumes everything it produces." [12] People on the large, southern Philippine island of Mindanao seem close to this description. The Mansakas, for example, hunt and cultivate crops, moving about as the soil is depleted. It is the women who clean the raw cotton and spin it into yarn. While the Mansakas are skilled weavers and dyers, producing their own colorful skirts, they do, however, purchase cloth for their blouses from traders.[13]

India is an example of a partly industrialized nation where until very recently the caste into which one was born determined his occupation. Time and changing conditions have served to loosen the caste system. In textile production, stiff competition from Japanese mills beginning in the early 1920s forced some hand-loom weavers to abandon their hereditary calling. Vestiges of the caste system remain today particularly in the lowest caste, the *harijans* or untouchables. Despite the fact that untouchability was abolished in the 1949 constitution and its practice is subject to criminal penalties, the untouchables, who number about 85 million and represent over one-seventh of the population, continue to work at the same hereditary caste-based occupations which include the skinning of dead animals and the tanning of hides.[14]

The U.S.S.R. and other communist countries are described as having command of centrally planned economies. Within the U.S.S.R. the amount of central planning varies with the particular good. Production and distribution of some goods are managed directly from Moscow; others are directed at the city council level. Reynolds describes the typical pattern of decision-making as follows. Policy decisions about the economy's growth rate, division of output between consumer and capital goods, pace of development, and distribution of plants among regions are made by the Council of Ministers of the U.S.S.R. The State Planning Commission turns the general directive into a detailed economic plan of production targets by republic. Republic officials make more detailed plans for each regional unit, and the regional councils appoint plant directors who are responsible for meeting the share of production assigned by the regional council.[15]

Textiles and clothing are among the controlled commodities and production and distribution take place within an elaborate system of agencies at various levels of the government. At the national level, the division of responsibility for cotton fiber production is illustrated by the fact that yields are a matter for the Ministry of Cotton

Growing, while the design of agricultural equipment falls within the domain of the Ministry of Agricultural Machine Building. Plans for fabric production are made in detail and include the size and location of plants and the quantities of specific fabrics to be produced. For example, information released by the Ministry of Cotton Growing in the mid-fifties indicated the following magnitudes of increase for specific types of fabric: 90 percent more cotton prints, 78 percent more sateen, and from two to seven percent more "dressy" fabrics, such as "artificial silk," velveteen, corduroy, taffeta and marquisette.[16]

Garments are designed by the All-Union Clothing Fashion House in Moscow and by similar fashion concerns in several dozen other cities. These establishments receive specially ordered fabrics from research institutes, and create designs for shows and exhibitions. They appear to be under the control of the local city administration, and the garments designed for production are appraised by an artistic council. Directors of retail concerns attend textile exhibitions and may choose designs and place orders with factories.

The All-Union Institute for Standards of Clothing and Light Industry Products, established under the State Planning Committee in 1959, has as one of its tasks the planning and coordination of fabric and apparel.[17] Articles in the Soviet press indicate that coordination is a problem.[18] *Izvestia*, for example, quoted the director of a specialized store as saying that "many millions of rubles are tied up in clothing that is 'not in demand' " because the tastes of the consumer are ignored. In 1960 this director selected 67 designs made of "stylish fabrics" at the All-Union Fashion House and placed an order for them with a factory in Moscow. However, only two of the designs were received because the factory did not ". . . turn out the new weaves and patterns of which the models were designed to be made and 'old and uninteresting' fabrics were used instead." [19] In the mid-60s the problem apparently remained because two clothing designers writing for *Izvestia* had this to say:

All the branches of light industry work in isolation from one another. The artistic councils for footwear, for fabrics, for clothing and for yard goods exist independently, and that is why all the goods are different in style and in character, why their colors do not go together, why many articles are missing altogether from the shops.[20]

The writers were of the opinion that this situation existed because designs were created without regard for the factories' raw materials and technical capabilities. The reluctance on the part of factories to introduce new lines occurred because their "plan-fulfillment indices," would be reduced and the intricate system of price formation would have to be adjusted, thus hindering and prolonging production.

Finally, there is also a system of quality control that includes product grading and inspection. Goods are inspected by factory personnel before leaving the factory. At the local Clothing Trade Trust warehouse the State Trade Inspector spot checks a small portion of the goods and those found defective are reduced in grade or returned to the factory for correction. The warehouse may levy fines against a factory for poor quality products, and the stores, in turn, may fine the warehouse if they are sent defective goods.[21]

In contrast to a centrally planned economy, the *market economy* is a system in which decisions are highly decentralized and are largely made by the private, as opposed to the government, sector. It is the individual who chooses, in accordance with his interests and abilities, the occupation he will enter and the geographic area in which he will work. Likewise, each business unit decides its line of production or distribution and determines what methods and materials are appropriate. Heilbroner points out that the operation of the system theoretically rests on the principle of self-interest and competition.[22] It is to the worker's advantage to seek the best remuneration attainable, and, therefore, it is possible to allocate workers for different economic activities by raising or lowering the rewards that the job offers. Businessmen also work in their own self-interest when they seek to make a profit while providing goods that the consumer will purchase. In a market economy consumer demand determines, to a large extent, what is produced. The economies of the U.S., Great Britain, and western European countries, which place a minimum of emphasis on tradition or central planning, are examples of the market economy.

How competition and self-interest affect distribution of workers in different jobs can be deduced from information on wages and characteristics of workers. Table 2 reports the average hourly gross earnings of U.S. workers in textile and apparel manufacturing and in all other manufacturing. It is readily seen that workers in the textile and apparel industries receive lower wages, on the average. This is undoubtedly related to the fact that the labor force in textile and apparel manufacturing, in contrast to all manufacturing, is characterized as having a higher median age, a higher proportion of women, a higher proportion of semi-skilled and lower proportion of skilled workers, lower median years of schooling and, in the apparel industry, a higher proportion of non-whites.[23]

Using the assets at its command, each apparel manufacturing establishment decides how it can best compete in pleasing a segment of the consumer market. Daves describes apparel manufacturing, suggesting a three category classification.[24] First are the prestige houses that emphasize quality of design and hand craftsmanship, produce a limited number of garments, and sell them for high prices. At an extreme opposite are companies that produce inexpensive, simplified designs in volume by using automated equipment as extensively as possible. Falling between these two is the most numerous group of manufacturers that produce clothing in a wide range of costliness and fashionability. Generally, the apparel is not as costly nor high fashion as that of the prestige houses or as standardized as that of the large automated company. Flexibility in meeting changing market demands is the asset of some of the smaller companies in this group.

Finally, clothing sales data give evidence of the consumer's influence on production. Consumer preference is not static and its changes have been one of the important factors, along with business cycles and import trends, in explaining sales phenomena. Recently, the quest for individuality among consumers has been credited with downgrading the role of the haute couture in fashion pace-setting, causing the industry to gear itself ". . . to provide an ever-widening spectrum of designs."[25]

TABLE 2.   Average hourly gross earnings.*

Period	All Manu-facturing	Textile Mill Products	Apparel and Related
1958	$2.11	$1.49	$1.54
1968	3.01	2.21	2.21
1970	3.36	2.45	2.40

* "Production Workers' Hours and Earnings," *Textile Hi-Lights* (Washington, D.C.: American Textile Manufacturers Institute, Inc.), March 1972, p. 23.

patterns of fiber
and apparel consumption

In this last section differences in patterns of fiber or apparel consumption will be noted. Three aspects of these patterns will be considered: quantity of fiber consumed, the proportionate use of different fibers, and the end use of fibers.

Quantity of Fiber Consumed

One of the difficulties in quantitative comparisons of consumption of goods from country to country is that of data representation. If consumption is expressed in units of value, a difficulty arises in equating currencies; if totals of weight or value are compared, population differences within countries are concealed; and if consumption is reported in quantities, quality differences in products are ignored. A partial solution has been to make comparisons on the basis of per capita, or per person, consumption, expressed in units of weight. While these per capita figures are not affected by currency differences and take into account the population of a country, they too may be misleading, for they are calculated by dividing total consumption of a product by total population. Therefore, each person is represented as receiving an equal share, while in fact the actual distribution patterns within a country may be quite unequal in both quantity and quality. Of particular difficulty in comparing clothing consumption is the unavailability of data on apparel consumption for all countries. As a result, information regarding fiber consumption must be used as a substitute. While the latter information is useful in indicating trends, it has the obvious disadvantage of imprecision regarding any one specific end use, such as apparel, home furnishings, or industrial uses.

With these limitations in mind we will consider the implications of per capita fiber consumption. Table 3 reveals how widely countries vary in this regard. In 1959-61 the developing countries consumed an average of 5.1 pounds of fiber per capita, compared with 18.9 pounds in developed regions other than the U.S., and 35.0 pounds in the United States. Projections for consumption in 1980 indicate gains for all countries, but the amount of gain varies greatly and will result in a widening of the gap between the lowest and highest consuming areas. For example, there was a 30.1 pound difference between the per capita consumption of India and the United States in 1959-61, but a 40 pound difference is projected for 1980. The U.S., already the world's largest consumer of fiber, will experience the largest increase, and the second highest ranked fiber consuming countries, Canada and Japan, are, by 1980, projected to attain the 35 pound per capita level that the U.S. reached 20 years earlier.[26]

Although many factors affect world fiber consumption, three of the major ones are population growth, which increases needs; consumer disposable income, which allows additional expenditures; and prices of other goods, which compete with fibers for the consumer's income. The data presented in Tables 3 and 4 are based on Food and Agriculture Organization of the United Nations (FAO) projections of a 1.5 to 3.2 annual percent increase in per capita income and a median rate of population growth.

TABLE 3.   Per capita fiber consumption for selected regions or countries.*

Country or region	1959–61 average	Projections for 1980	Per capita lbs. increase
	lbs.	lbs.	lbs.
World	11.2	14.1	2.9
Foreign Free World **	9.6	11.7	2.1
Centrally Planned Countries **	9.6	12.2	2.6
United States	35.0	54.0	19.0
Developed regions excluding the U.S.	18.9	27.7	8.8
Canada	24.9	35.0	10.1
Japan	22.8	35.0	12.2
Developing regions	5.1	5.8	.7
People's Republic of China	5.2	5.3	.1
India	4.9	6.0	1.1

* *Cotton and Other Fiber Problems and Policies in the United States* (Washington, D.C.: U.S. Government Printing Office, National Advisory Committee on Food and Fiber), Technical Papers, II (July, 1967), 58–60, 63.
** "Centrally planned countries" include the U.S.S.R., eastern European countries, and the People's Republic of China. "Foreign free world" includes the remaining foreign countries.

Proportionate Consumption of Fibers

The proportion in which different fibers are consumed also varies from one country to another. While cotton accounted for the largest share of fiber consumption in each of the countries, its use was much more dominant in developing countries where it accounted for an average of 86 percent of the total in 1959-1961. Man-made fibers, as shown in Table 4, represented only 10 percent of the total consumption in developing countries compared with 28 percent in developed nations. Projections for 1980 indicate cotton will remain the dominant fiber for developing countries, although its share will decline slightly, and in developed countries man-made fibers will have a slight percentage edge over cotton.

TABLE 4. **Fiber consumption as percentages * of total for selected regions or countries.** **

Country or region	1959–1961				Projected for 1980			
	Natural		Man-made		Natural		Man-made	
	Cotton	Wool	Cellulosic	Synthetic	Cotton	Wool	Cellulosic	Synthetic
World	68	10	18	4	52	6	17	24
Foreign Free World	65	11	19	5	54	7	16	22
Centrally Planned	76	8	15	1	57	6	21	16
United States	65	8	17	10	41	5	14	40
Developed Regions excluding the U.S.	59	14	23	5	44	9	21	26
Canada	56	12	23	10	37	9	19	35
Japan	51	12	26	11	35	7	18	40
Developing Regions	86	4	8	2	76	3	12	9
People's Republic of China	96	2	2	—	76	2	13	9
India	92	2	6	—	86	1.5	8	5.5

* Percentages may not add to 100 because of rounding.
** *Cotton and Other Fiber Problems and Policies in the United States.* (Washington, D.C.: U.S. Government Printing Office, National Advisory Committee on Food and Fiber), Technical Papers, II, (July, 1967), 63.

End Uses of Fibers

The third aspect of the consumption pattern that varies is the proportion of fiber that is allocated to the apparel end use. "The great bulk of fiber consumed in low income countries is made into clothing," while in developed or high income countries ". . . nonapparel uses account for a substantial proportion of the demand . . ." [27] In 1967-68, 60 percent of the fiber consumed in western Europe and 62 percent of that consumed in the U.S.S.R. and eastern Europe went for the apparel end use. In the U.S. a smaller share of total fiber, 40 percent, was used in clothing in 1967-68. [28]

summary

All societies have a similar economic problem: the demand for economic goods, those made from scarce resources, increases as population increases and as human expectations rise. Clothing and accessories which cover and ornament the body are among the economic goods that are demanded. A nation's economic system provides a mechanism for allotting scarce resources among possible end uses, for organizing the production and distribution of goods, and for distributing income to individuals. The particular economic system of a society, along with its resource endowment and population/resource ratio, influence the production of goods within that society. Consumption patterns are influenced by income distribution and by the quantity, variety, and price of available goods. Fiber and apparel consumption patterns differ from society to society because of the interplay of all these factors.

13

ONE WORLD OF DRESS

dress and basic human concerns

Individuals throughout the world have similar biological, aesthetic, and social concerns when covering and ornamenting their bodies. These concerns are the focus of basic divisions of this book.

Biological Concerns

The biological needs of the body must be considered in relation to climate and geography since in all environments these factors influence the dress people wear. However, climate and geography do not determine the exact type or amount of clothing that will be worn in any given environmental situation. Alternatives exist. On a short-term basis acclimatization of the body to a particular climate may

210

occur and modify clothing needs. On a long-term basis, that is after many generations, genetic changes may also alter clothing needs. In addition, in cold climates caloric intake may be increased to generate more body heat or, as an alternative, housing with auxiliary heating systems may be introduced. Air conditioning moderates tropical heat. As temperatures are controlled in houses, schools, factories, stores, offices, airplanes, and motor vehicles around the world, needs for different weights of clothes and different numbers of layers of clothes decrease.

Aesthetic Concerns

Presenting the body in an aesthetically pleasing way is another common concern in all societies. Cultural ideals for beauty evolve for both body and dress, and individuals generally select dress that approximates the ideal within their own society. Sometimes more than one ideal exists within a society, especially in the society that is characterized by great heterogeneity in physical types as well as

Fig. 13–1. The Lapps in Scandinavia and North American Eskimo dress themselves for protection against extreme cold, but the decorative elements of their clothing are quite different. (Courtesy of (a) *Vanishing Peoples*, p. 54, photograph by George Mobley, © 1969 National Geographic Society; (b) Information Canada Phototheque.)

(a)   (b)

ideology. Also subcultural ideals for beauty can exist for groups that are set apart from the general society on some basis, such as age, ethnic differences, or religion.

Social Concerns

People in all societies also develop some kind of social orientations toward dress. These orientations are associated with the type of society in which they live, whether traditional (folk or agrarian) or industrial (urban-industrial or mass). In the traditional societies people will be ruled by custom and accept custom as a guide in making decisions on how to dress. Those in industrial societies will be more oriented to change and may make a virtue of change within an established fashion system. Dress serves as a means of societal communication among all people but what the forms of dress are and what their meanings are will depend upon the unique combination of cultural characteristics of each society.

Interaction Among Basic Concerns

Biological, aesthetic, and social concerns interact with each other in multiple ways in the determination of types of dress. As a result, groups of people, and individuals within groups, can arrive at very dissimilar appearing dress. For example, the Lapps in Scandinavia and the Eskimo of North America dress themselves for protection against extreme cold, but the decorative expression of their apparel is quite different.

similarities and differences in dress

Independent Development of Forms of Dress

Similar general solutions of how to construct dress for the human body have been reached worldwide in apparently independent origin. However, differences occur in the interpretation of basic forms, types of materials used, methods of decoration, design motifs used, and meanings attached to the total form or details within the total form. The basic forms of dress were presented in Chapter Six as reconstructing, enclosing (including wraparound, suspended, fitted, and combination variations), and attached. As far as we know, the Indian sari, the West African wrapper, and the Samoan *lavalava* developed independently of each other, yet each is a wraparound garment worn in approximately the same general way. Similarly, peoples in widely scattered parts of the world have devised ways of utilizing natural pigments to paint their bodies, and methods of tattooing designs on their skin.

Borrowed Forms of Dress

Although some forms of clothing and adornment seem to have been thought of by people independent of contact with other groups, many forms of clothing and adornment are similar because human beings have had contact with other groups of humans during their lifetimes. In times past, small folk groups had contact with neighboring groups. Today, since contact is widespread and made common by the ease of air travel, ideas for dress are easily transferred from country to country and continent to continent. American youth, traveling extensively as private citizens and as members of organized endeavors such as the Peace Corps and Crossroads Africa, have helped popularize casual dress, such as blue jeans, with other young people around the world. For example, a reporter for the *New York Times* in Moscow wrote that he had seen a long-haired Russian youth in a theatre lobby wearing blue jeans and a button-down shirt.[1] The Yoruba people from Nigeria have contributed the "dashiki" (or *danshiki* as it is known in Yoruba) to black Americans, as part of the "Afro" look that has developed in the United States. From a different part of the world, South America, has come the poncho, which has enjoyed popularity in both the United States and Europe. The Eskimo parka, with its functional aspects, has been borrowed in other parts of the world for protection from the cold. The Western business suit has become accepted in many parts of the world as expected men's wear in the commercial and professional world, while caftans and burnooses of Middle Eastern men have been borrowed by women in the West for leisure wear. Kimonos have also been adapted for leisure-wear use in the West, particularly by women.

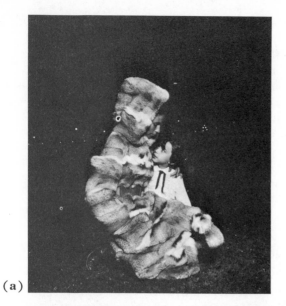

(a)

(b)

(c)

Fig. 13–2. (a) Parkas, based on Eskimo designs, are worn in many parts of the world; (b) burnoose designs from the Middle East have been used as inspiration for women's leisure wear in the West; and (c) the kimono design has been adapted for leisure wear in the West. (Courtesy of (a) *Vogue,* copyright 1968 by The Condé Nast Publications Inc., and (b) and (c) Celanese®.)

Industrialization and Forms of Dress

Similarities in forms of dress around the world are also occurring because of the prevalence of industrialization. Thus in only a few isolated areas, where industrialization has not touched or had significant impact, are traditional costumes still worn. For example, one author claims that in the Western hemisphere only in Bolivia, Ecuador, Peru and a few places in Mexico and Guatemala are typical costumes with traditional elements still worn daily.[2] When industrialization occurs, an advanced technology develops for spinning, weaving, cutting, and sewing; and mass production of clothing results in fabrics and clothing becoming cheaper to produce. Studies of culture around the world indicate that when industrialization occurs and cost is lessened, fabrics become less prized as artifacts and cutting into fabric to make fitted garments becomes more common practice. In many traditional societies handmade cloth is not cut into perhaps because the textile itself is valued. For example, handwoven and gold embroidered sari cloth has an intrinsic value that industrially produced blue denim does not have.

Industrialization brings rural people to the city to work in the factory and thereby encourages clustering of populations in large urban areas. It also fosters development of an elaborate occupational structure with bureaucracies typically developed for organiz-

Fig. 13–3.   Japanese school girls in Western dress. (Courtesy of Lenore Landry.)

ing personnel. The office workers in the bureaucracies as well as factory workers and school children seem to prefer the "practicality" of Western garb for their occupational and educational pursuits. The kimono in Japan has been rejected in factories because it is felt to be unsafe.[3] Men appear to adopt Western dress faster than women, probably because they adopt industrial jobs faster than women who maintain traditional work roles. However, when men have traditional jobs, they also wear traditional dress as in the case of the Taiwanese rice paddy farmer who wears traditional dress and high wooden clogs, which keep his feet dry. Thus the important relationship between "Western" dress and industrialization may not be the male and female difference but the difference between individuals, male or female, who work at industrial or traditional tasks.[4] Typically, traditional tasks are characteristic of rural areas, thus traditional dress is frequently found in rural places and Western garments in urban places. Traditional rulers also are likely to wear traditional dress. Thus the complexity of a developing country may be seen in the diversity of the dress of its people.

Similar forms of dress have also become more widely available around the world because of modern transportation and mass communications systems. In the 1960s and 1970s news of styles such as

Fig. 13–4. The complexity of a developing country may be seen in the diversity of the dress of its people (graduation day at the University of Ibadan). (Courtesy of the Federal Ministry of Information, Lagos, Nigeria.)

Fig. 13–5. Modern transportation and mass communication systems help bring Western fashion changes to remote places like the jungle of interior Brazil. (Courtesy of John Dominis, Time/Life Syndication Service.)

the "mini," the "midi," and "hot pants" was widely disseminated through international magazines and on television to places quite far from their origins. For example, as a new highway was being cut through the Brazilian jungle, to the interior of Brazil, photographers for *Life* magazine brought back photographs of women in that interior wearing "hot pants" and boots, the latest fashion at that time.[5]

Finally, industrialization usually brings with it increased personal income which allows individuals the chance of purchasing more apparel items as well as becoming involved in a way of life in which specialized clothing is associated with specialized activities. Some of the greatest specialization can be seen in many sports and activities that require special costumes: swimming, skiing, tennis, ice skating, fencing, snowmobiling, and hunting, for example. Special organizations such as scouting and fraternal orders often require specialized dress.

(a)   **(b)**

Fig. 13–6. Specialization in dress particularly noticeable in sports that require special costumes. (Courtesy of (a) John Brubaker, and (b) Celanese®.)

Fig. 13–7. Specialized organizations such as scouting and fraternal orders often require specialized dress. (Courtesy of Celanese®.)

Reasons for Borrowing Forms of Dress

How do we explain why some forms of dress are borrowed from other people while other forms have been ignored? First, admiration for another society and its way of life may account for the acceptance of clothing items from that group of people. Frequently, emerging nations have copied the "successful" Western world and its way of dress. It was common in the 1950s and 1960s, for example, for Africans who were educated abroad in Europe and America to prefer the Western-type garments they had become accustomed to wearing during their time of schooling. By the late 1960s, however, indigenous dress in countries like Nigeria had again become popular and was seen side-by-side with Western garments. The Masai have been urged, even forced by law, to wear trousers to indicate to the rest of the world, especially tourists, that Tanzania is modern.[6] Even Russian women have copied the Western fashion of pantsuits. As one observer reported:

In clothing the West is still looked to. Pants suits have become the rage of Moscow in recent months and have spread to the provinces as well. So far they are made at home or in tailor shops; regular stores do not stock them, much to the annoyance of women whose complaints have been printed in the press.[7]

Fig. 13–8. Admiration for another society and its way of life may account for acceptance of clothing items. A Mossi from Upper Volta is shown wearing a secondhand sweatshirt. (Courtesy of National Geographic Society, photograph by Bruce Dale, © August 1966 by National Geographic Society.)

Fig. 13–9. In the United States the Krishna people are a religious sect that has taken on aspects of Hindu dress as well as religion. (Courtesy of Jeff Wilner.)

Fig. 13–10. A Nigerian market stall in which second-hand clothes are being sold. (Courtesy of Joanne B. Eicher.)

Western fashions are not always looked to as the desirable: some individuals in Western societies have rejected the Western garb which is native to them and have begun to copy the clothing of people of other countries or of earlier times. Some of the religious sects in the United States, such as the Krishna people, have taken on a Hindu way of dress as well as aspects of the Hindu religion, and North American youth have borrowed American Indian items of dress or calico dresses of the frontier days of the United States, perhaps expressing admiration for a simpler way of life. Even those individuals who do not reject Western fashion may find themselves admiring items of clothing from other cultures because they represent the hand work of the skilled craftsman rather than the standardized, impersonal products of the machine, so easily available. Thus handmade sandals from India or Mexico, handwoven textiles from Ghana or Navajo country become prized objects to wear or display even though in their indigenous settings they may be commonplace and not valued.

The worldwide distribution of second-hand items of Western dress also fosters borrowing of Western forms. Since second-hand clothing is frequently less expensive than domestically produced new clothing, it may be all that people can afford to buy. Although little has been written about the economics of the second-hand clothing business, a brisk trade exists from America and Northern Europe to many of the emerging nations. Complete outfits of clothing can be purchased on the retail second-hand market for the equivalent of no more than two or three American dollars.

dress in the future

As more of the world mechanizes and industrializes, the technology for volume manufacturing of cloth and clothing will promote similar forms of dress. In addition, as we conquer our environment with the technology of space and the underwater world, the forms needed for clothing in those hostile environments will be extremely similar; for no matter what the cultural background of the person going to the moon or deepsea diving, support of physiological functioning is a foremost factor influencing design—aesthetic and social concerns are secondary. The trend toward control of world environment with air-conditioning and central heating is also likely to encourage widespread use of similar types of dress.

Frequently, designers, philosophers, and others interested in dress forecast fashions of the future. For example, designer Rudi Gernreich has sketched skirts, pants, and leotard outfits which he predicts adult males and females, with physically fit bodies, will wear during the 1970s. In addition he has proposed that colorful caftans will be worn by old people to cover the ugliness of their aging bodies.[8]

Another designer, John Weitz, has predicted that in the year 2068 we will live in a temperature controlled, dirt-free environment and will not have to consider seasonal changes in selecting our clothing. Therefore, both men and women will wear two one-piece garments, one called "unders" which combines the features of under-

Fig. 13–11. Designer Rudi Gernreich sketched skirts and leotard outfits which he predicts will be worn in the 1970s.

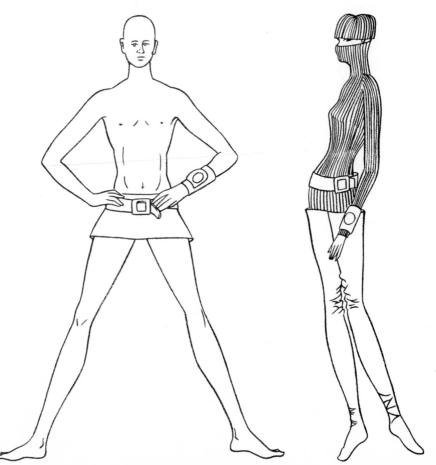

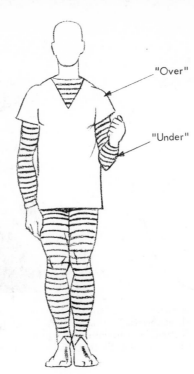

"Over"

"Under"

Fig. 13–12. For the second half of the twenty-first century, John Weitz predicts that two layers of garments will be typical, one layer as underwear, and one layer as a decorative status garment.

garments presently worn and one called "overs" which will be decorative and used as a status symbol.[9]

Whether or not we can predict the exact details of dress of the future, we can project the most likely possibilities for clothing based on current technological developments. Natural fibers have been decreasing in use in proportion to synthetic fibers in apparel. If this trend continues, the woven garment made of any natural fiber,

Fig. 13–13. Many clothing and other dress items made of synthetic fibers are likely to be molded into shape rather than cut and sewn. (Courtesy of *Textile World* and the Van Dyck Corporation.)

Garment-making with laser and holography

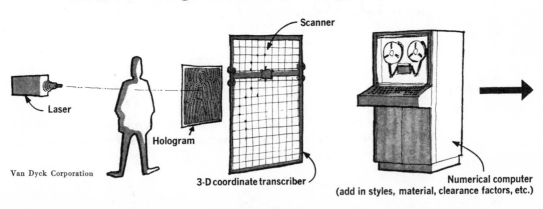

Van Dyck Corporation

Laser

Hologram

Scanner

3-D coordinate transcriber

Numerical computer (add in styles, material, clearance factors, etc.)

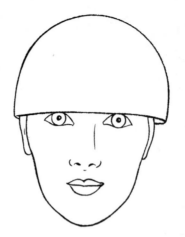

Fig. 13–14. Similarities among very different peoples in different parts of the world may occur. Rudi Gernreich predicts helmet-shaped Dynel wigs for the future which are similar in appearance to the traditional headdress of Warra males in Brazil. (Warra headdress courtesy of Vilma Chiara Schultz. Photograph by Harald Schultz.)

whether wool, silk, linen, or cotton, may become rare and prized for special-occasion wear. Many clothing and other dress items made of synthetic fibers are likely to be molded into shape rather than cut and sewn. Items that are standardized and easy to dispense may be sold from vending machines just as certain items of cosmetics are sold today in transportation stations for travelers.

Human beings have consistently through history sought individuality, and decorative variations of forms of dress appear to be unlimited; therefore, complete uniformity in dress is unlikely. However, because there are only limited basic forms of dress, people with very different cultural backgrounds in widely-scattered parts of the world may exhibit similarities in dress. Some counter movements may add to distinctions in dress. For example, if emerging nations become disenchanted with the Western world, trends toward distinctive "national" dress, as have already been seen in Africa, may be encouraged.

summary

For all people, the kind of dress they wear is related to biological, aesthetic, and social concerns. However, their dress can differ a great deal because of variations in physical environment, resources available, cultural ideals for beauty, social values, personal philosophies, industrial developments, and degree of isolation from other people.

As efficient production, transportation, and communication systems of the twentieth century make similar items of dress familiar to and available to people around the world, a move toward one world of dress evolves. However, since distinctions in dress have long been valued, many individuals and groups are likely to continue striving for distinct identities via dress, despite developing world unity. And variations in dress are likely to remain available, even when choices are made among standardized, mass-produced products; for machines can also turn out many types of products rapidly. Distinction can be achieved by choosing among a number of alternate items of dress and combining them in unique ways.

NOTES

Chapter 1   [1] "Modern Stone-Age Men," *Science News*, XCVI (December 20, 1969), 583; "Paleolithic Funeral," *Scientific American*, CCXII, No. 2 (February, 1965), 53–54.

[2] H. C. BROHOLM and MARGRETHE HALD, *Costumes of the Bronze Age in Denmark* (Copenhagen: Nyt Nordisk Forlag, 1940).

[3] STEFAN LORANT, *The New World* (New York: Duell, Sloan & Pearce, 1946), p. 31. John White's watercolors were published for the first time in this 1946 book which also contains reprints of Theodore DeBry's engravings from both White's and Jacques Demorgues' paintings.

[4] MILLIA DAVENPORT, *The Book of Costume* (New York: Crown Publishers, 1948), Vol. II, 485.

[5] VYVIAN HOLLAND, *Hand Coloured Fashion Plates 1770 to 1899* (London: B. T. Batsford Ltd., 1955), pp. 21–22.

[6] "Postage Stamps with Textile Motifs," Ciba Review, No. 2, 1970, 10–30.

[7] *Travels of Marco Polo* (New York: Orion Press, 1958), p. 57.

[8] CAPTAIN W. J. L. WHARTON, ed., *Captain Cook's Journal During His First Voyage Around the World Made in H. M. Bark "Endeavour" 1768–71* (London: Elliot Stock, 1893), p. 93.

[9] FRANCES TROLLOPE, *Domestic Manners of Americans* (New York: Alfred A. Knopf, 1949), pp. 299–300.

[10] THOMAS HOPE, *Costume of the Ancients* (London: Henry G. Bohn, 1841, 1st ed. 1809); JAMES R. PLANCHE, *History of British Costume* (London: C. Cox, 1847, 1st ed. 1834); HERMANN WEISS, *Geschichte des Kostüms* (Berlin: F. Dümmler, 1853), and *Kostümkunde* (Stuttgart: Ebner und Seubert, 1860–72); F. W. FAIRHOLT, *Costume in England* (London: Chapman and Hall, 1846).

[11] J. QUICHERAT, *Histoire du costume en France depuis les. temps les plus reculés jusqu'a la fin du XVIII siècle* (Paris: Librairie Hachette et Cie, 1877); ALBERT CHARLES AUGUSTE RACINET, *Le Costume Historique* (Paris: Firmin-Didot, 1888); FR. HOTTENROTH, *Le Costume Chez les Peuples Anciens et Modernes* (Paris: Armand Guerinet, 189–?); CARL ROHRBACH, *Die Trachten der Volker vom Beginn der Geschichte bis zum neunzehnten Jahrhundert gezeichnet* (trans. The Costume of All Nations from the Earliest Times to the Nineteenth Century); lithographs by A. Kretschmer (London: Henry Sothern and Co., 1882).

[12] CHARLES FABRI, *A History of Indian Dress* (Calcutta: Orient Longmans, 1960, 1961); G. S. GHURYE, *Indian Costume* (Bombay: Popular Prakashan, 1951); HELEN BENTON MINNICH, *Japanese Costume* (Rutland, Vermont: Charles E. Tuttle Company, 1963); JOSEPHINE WOOD and LILLY DE JONGH OSBORNE, *Indian Costumes of Guatemala* (Graz, Austria: Akademische Dracku. Verlagsanstalt, 1966); A. C. SCOTT, *Chinese Costume in Transition* (Singapore: Donald Moore, 1958); S. M. MEAD, *Traditional Maori Clothing* (Auckland: A. H. and A. W. Reed, 1969); DONALD CORDRY and DOROTHY CORDRY, *Mexican Indian Costumes* (Austin: University of Texas Press, 1968); WALTER A. FAIRSERVIS, JR., *Costumes of the East* (Riverside, Conn.: The Chatham Press, Inc., 1971).

[13] DAVENPORT, *op. cit.*

[14] FRANCOIS BOUCHER, *A History of Costume in the West* (London: Thames and Hudson, 1967); BLANCHE PAYNE, *History of Costume* (New York: Harper & Row, 1965).

Chapter 2

[1] PHILIP STUBS, *The Anatomie of Abuses* (London: Richard Johnes, 1595), p. 8.

[2] CLAY GEERDES, "I'm Ugly and I'm Proud," *Kaleidoscope,* October 1, 1969, p. 5.

[3] THOMAS CARLYLE, *Sartor Resartus* (New York: The Odyssey Press, 1937), pp. 72–73. First edition in book form in 1834.

[4] ARTHUR M. SCHLESINGER, *Learning How to Behave* (New York: The Macmillan Company, 1947), p. 18.

[5] MRS. E. G. DUFFEY, *Our Behavior, a Manual of Etiquette and Dress of the Best American Society* (Philadelphia: J. M. Stoddard and Company, 1876), pp. 3–4.

[6] EMILY POST, *Etiquette, the Blue Book of Social Usage* (New York: Funk and Wagnalls Company, 1928), p. 597. First published in 1922.

[7] MRS. MERRIFIELD, *Dress as a Fine Art* (London: Author Hall, Virture and Co., 1854), p. 93.

[8] *Decorum* (New York: J. A. Ruth and Co., 1879), p. 270.

[9] LILLIAN EICHLER, *Book of Etiquette*, 2 vols. (Oyster Bay, N. Y.: Nelson Doubleday, Inc., 1921); POST, *op. cit.* Schlesinger reports that by 1945 over a million copies of Lillian Eichler's book had been sold and over two-thirds of a million of Emily Post's. Schlesinger, *op. cit.*, p. 51.

[10] HAYDEN NORWOOD, *Common Sense Etiquette Dictionary* (Emaus, Penn.: Rodale Publications, Inc., 1937), p. 7.

[11] GRACE MORTON, *The Arts of Costume and Personal Appearance*, 3rd ed. rev. (New York: John Wiley and Sons, 1964), pp. 42, 238.

[12] HELEN G. CHAMBERS and VERNA MOULTON, *Clothing Selection: Fashions, Figures, Fabrics*, 2nd ed. (Philadelphia: J. B. Lippincott Company, 1969), p. 230.

[13] MRS. MERRIFIELD, *op. cit.*, p. 93; MARIETTA KETTUNEN, *Fundamentals of Dress* (New York: McGraw-Hill Book Co., 1941), pp. 47–57; JOAN O'SULLIVAN, *How to Be Well Dressed* (Garden City, N. Y.: Nelson Doubleday, Inc., 1969), p. 14.

[14] DOROTHY STOTE, *Men Too Wear Clothes* (New York: Frederick A. Stockes Company, 1939).

[15] GABRIEL TARDE, *The Laws of Imitation*, trans. by Elsie Clews Parsons (New York: Henry Holt and Company, 1903); GUSTAVE LE BON, *The Crowd* (London: T. Fischer Unwin Ltd., 1895).

[16] RICHARD VON KRAFFT-EBING, *Psychopathia Sexualis* (New York: Bell Publishing Company, Inc., 1965), (1st ed. Stuttgart, 1886); SIGMUND FREUD, *The Interpretation of Dreams* (New York: The Macmillan Co., 1915, 1st ed. 1900); HAVELOCK ELLIS, *Studies in the Psychology of Sex* (New York: The Modern Library, Inc., 1936), I and II.

[17] SIGMUND FREUD, *A General Introduction to Psychoanalysis* (Garden City, N. Y.: Garden City Publishing Company, 1943), pp. 135–44. (From lectures presented 1915–1917.)

[18] WILLIAM THOMAS, *Sex and Society* (Chicago: The University of Chicago Press, 1907), pp. 201–20.

[19] EDWARD A. ROSS, *Social Psychology* (New York: The Macmillan Company, 1908).

[20] GEORG SIMMEL, "Fashion," *International Quarterly*, X (October, 1904), pp. 130–55.

[21] THORSTEIN VEBLEN, *The Theory of the Leisure Class* (New York: The Macmillan Company, 1899).

[22] WILFRED MARK WEBB, *The Heritage of Dress* (London: The Times Book Club, 1912, 1st ed. 1907).

[23] A. E. CRAWLEY, "Dress," *Encyclopaedia of Religion and Ethics*, ed. James Hastings (New York: Charles Scribner's Sons, 1912), V, 40–72.

[24] GEORGE VAN NESS DEARBORN, "The Psychology of Clothing," *The Psychological Monographs*, XXVI, No. 1 (1918), 1–72.

[25] L. H. NEWBURGH, ed., *Physiology of Heat Regulation and the Science of Clothing* (Philadelphia: W. B. Saunders Company, 1949). Reprint, New York: Hafner Publishing Company, Inc., 1968.

[26] LYMAN FOURT and NORMAN R. S. HOLLIES, *Clothing: Comfort and Function* (New York: Marcel Dekker, Inc., 1970).

[27] E. T. RENBOURN, *Materials and Clothing in Health and Disease* (London: H. K. Lewis & Co. Ltd., 1972).

[28] YEHUDI A. COHEN, *Man in Adaptation: The Biosocial Background* (Chicago: Aldine Publishing Company, 1968).

[29] HILAIRE HILER, *From Nudity to Raiment* (New York: E. Weyhe, 1929).

[30] ELIZABETH B. HURLOCK, *The Psychology of Dress* (New York: The Ronald Press Company, 1929); J. C. FLUGEL, *The Psychology of Clothes* (London: The Hogarth Press, Ltd., 1930).

[31] PAUL H. NYSTROM, *Economics of Fashion* (New York: The Ronald Press Company, 1928).

[32] RUTH BENEDICT, "Dress," *Encyclopaedia of the Social Sciences* (New York: The Macmillan Company, 1931), V, 235–37; RUTH BUNZEL, "Ornament," *Encyclopaedia of the Social Sciences, op. cit.*, XI, 496–97; EDWARD SAPIR, "Fashion," *Encyclopaedia of the Social Sciences, op. cit.*, VI, 139–44.

[33] ERNEST CRAWLEY, *Dress, Drinks, and Drums*, ed. by Theodore Besterman (London: Methuen & Co., Ltd., 1931), pp. 1–175.

[34] HILAIRE HILER and MEYER HILER, *Bibliography of Costume* (New York: The H.W. Wilson Company, 1939).

[35] RENÉ COLAS, *Bibliographie Générale du Costume et de la Mode* (Paris:

R. Colas, 1933); ISABEL STEVENSON MONRO and DOROTHY E. COOK, *Costume Index* (New York: The H. W. Wilson Company, 1937; supplement, 1957).

[36] FRANZ JOSEPH LIPPERHEIDE, *Katalog der Freiherrlich von Lipperheideshen Kostümbibliothek* (Berlin: F. Lipperheide, 1896–1905).

[37] C. W. CUNNINGTON, *Why Women Wear Clothes* (London: Faber and Faber, 1941); QUENTIN BELL, *On Human Finery* (London: The Hogarth Press, 1947).

[38] ELIZABETH HAWES, *Fashion Is Spinach* (New York: Random House, 1938); *It's Still Spinach* (Boston: Little, Brown and Company, 1954); BERNARD RUDOFSKY, *Are Clothes Modern?* (Chicago: Paul Theobald, 1947). An updated version is titled *The Unfashionable Human Body* (Garden City: Doubleday and Company, Inc., 1971).

[39] W. H. SHELDON, *The Varieties of Human Physique* (New York: Harper and Brothers, 1940); W. H. SHELDON, *The Varieties of Temperament* (New York: Harper and Brothers, 1942).

[40] JAMES LAVER, *Museum Piece* (Boston: Houghton Mifflin Co., 1964), p. 242; and *Clothes* (London: Burke, 1952).

[41] EDMUND BERGER, *Fashion and the Unconscious* (New York: Robert Brunner, 1953).

[42] LAWRENCE LANGNER, *The Importance of Wearing Clothes* (New York: Hastings House, 1959).

[43] JAMES LAVER, *Clothes*, op. cit., pp. ix–xv; JAMES LAVER, *Modesty in Dress* (Boston: Houghton Mifflin Co., 1969), p. 33.

[44] G. P. STONE, "Appearance and the Self," in *Human Behavior and Social Processes: An Interactionist Approach*, ed. A. M. Rose (New York: Houghton Mifflin Co., 1962), pp. 86–118.

[45] MARY ELLEN ROACH and JOANNE BUBOLZ EICHER, eds., *Dress, Adornment and the Social Order* (New York: John Wiley and Sons, Inc., 1965).

[46] MARY S. RYAN, *Clothing, A Study in Human Behavior* (New York: Holt, Rinehart & Winston, 1966).

[47] KARLYNE ANSPACH, *The Why of Fashion* (Ames, Iowa: Iowa State University Press, 1967.

[48] MARILYN J. HORN, *The Second Skin* (Boston: Houghton Mifflin Co., 1968).

[49] HERBERT BLUMER, "Fashion," *International Encyclopaedia of the Social Sciences*, ed. David L. Sills (New York: The Macmillan Company & The Free Press, 1968), V. 341–45.

[50] ORRIN E. KLAPP, *Collective Search for Identity* (New York: Holt, Rinehart & Winston, 1969).

51 Mary Lou Rosencranz, *Clothing Concepts: A Social-Psychological Approach* (New York: The Macmillan Company, 1972).

52 René König, *Kleider und Leute, Zur Soziologie der Mode* (Frankfurt: Fischer Bücherei, 1967); Ingrid Brenninkmeyer, *The Sociology of Fashion* (Winterthur: P. G. Keller, 1963).

53 S. M. Mead, *Traditional Maori Clothing* (Auckland: A. H. and A. W. Reed, 1969).

54 Andrew Strathern and Marilyn Strathern, *Self-Decoration in Mount Hagan* (London: Gerald Duckworth and Co. Ltd., 1971).

55 Petr Bogatyrev, *The Functions of Folk Costume in Moravian Slovakia* (Paris: Mouton, 1971).

56 Joanne Bubolz Eicher, *African Dress: A Select and Annotated Bibliography of Subsaharan Countries* (East Lansing, Michigan: Michigan State University, 1970).

Chapter 3

1 Ernest L. Schusky and T. Patrick Culbert, *Introducing Culture* (Englewood Cliffs, New Jersey: Prentice-Hall, Inc., 1967), p. 61.

2 Alice Brues, "The Spearman and the Archer," *American Anthropologist*, LXI, No. 3 (June 1959), 457–69.

3 James F. Downs and Herman K. Bleibtreu, *Human Variation*, rev. ed. (Beverly Hills, California: Glencoe Press, 1972), p. 304.

4 *Ibid*, pp. 266–67.

5 Many generalizations about skin color, hair color and texture, and eye color can be found in basic anthropological references. One typical source is Sonia Cole, *Races of Man* (London: British Museum, 1963), pp. 20–24.

6 *Ibid*, p. 24.

7 Downs and Bleibtreu, *op. cit.*, pp. 262–63.

8 Cole, *op. cit.*, p. 25.

9 W. H. Sheldon, *The Varieties of Human Physique* (New York: Harper and Brothers, 1940), pp. 1–5.

10 Downs and Bleibtreu, *op. cit.*, p. 310.

Chapter 4

1 "The Physiology and Hygiene of Clothes," *Ciba Review*, IV (1964), 26.

2 *Man, Sweat, and Performance* (Rutherford, New Jersey: Consumer Products Division, Becton, Dickinson and Company, 1969), p. 11.

3 *Ibid*, p. 21.

4 *Ibid*, p. 20.

[5] CARLETON S. COON, *The Origin of Races* (New York: Alfred A. Knopf, 1962), p. 70.

[6] CARLOS M. MONGE, "Man, Climate, and Changes of Altitude," in Yehudi A. Cohen, *Man in Adaptation: The Bio-social Background* (Chicago: Aldine Publishing Company, 1968), pp. 176–85.

[7] CARLETON S. COON, STANLEY M. GARN, and JOSEPH B. BIRDSELL, "Adaptive Changes in the Human Body," in E. Adamson Hoebel, Jesse D. Jennings, and Elmer R. Smith, eds., *Readings in Anthropology* (New York: McGraw-Hill Book Company, Inc., 1955), p. 101.

[8] COON, *op. cit.*, pp. 63–67.

[9] LYMAN FOURT and NORMAN R. S. HOLLIES, *Clothing, Comfort and Function* (New York: Marcel Dekker, Inc., 1970), p. 31.

[10] PHILIP K. BOCK, *Modern Cultural Anthropology* (New York: Alfred A. Knopf, 1969), pp. 255–57.

[11] HAROLD E. DRIVER, *Indians of North America* 2nd ed. rev. (Chicago: University of Chicago Press, 1969), p. 151.

[12] KAJ BIRKET-SMITH, *The Paths of Culture* (Madison: The University of Wisconsin Press, 1965), pp. 215–16.

[13] FREDERICK A. MILAN, *Swedish Lappland: A Brief Description of the Dwellings and Winter-Living Techniques of the Swedish Mountain Lapps,* Arctic Aeromedical Laboratory, TR 60–7 (October, 1960), p. 12.

[14] "Man Amplifier," *Newsweek*, LIII, No. 22 (June 1, 1964), p. 47.

[15] PAUL A. SIPLE, "Clothing and Climate," in L. H. Newburgh, ed., *Physiology of Heat Regulation and the Science of Clothing* (New York: Hafner Publishing Co., 1968), p. 389.

[16] FOURT and HOLLIES, *op. cit.*, p. 23.

[17] PHILLIP V. TOBIAS, "Bushman Hunter-Gatherers: A Study in Human Ecology," in Yehudi A. Cohen, ed., *Man in Adaptation: The Biosocial Background* (Chicago: Aldine Publishing Company, 1968), p. 205.

[18] *Ibid*, p. 205.

[19] SIPLE, *op, cit.*, p. 403.

[20] BOCK, *op, cit.*, p. 239; and ERNA GUNTHER, *Art in the Life of the Northwest Coast Indian* (Portland, Oregon: The Portland Art Museum, 1966), pp. 56–61.

[21] SIPLE, *op. cit.*, pp. 438–39.

[22] S. J. KENNEDY and JAN H. VANDERLIE, "Enhancing the Effectiveness of the Individual in the Arctic Through Clothing and Equipment," *Review of Research on Military Problems in Cold Regions*, Arctic Aeromedical Laboratory, TD 64–28, December, 1964, p. 137.

[23] L. H. Newburgh, ed., *Physiology of Heat Regulation and the Science of Clothing* (Philadelphia: W. B. Saunders Company, 1949), pp. 9–10. Reprints New York: Hafner Publishing Company, Inc., 1968.

[24] For more details see: Richard S. Johnston, James V. Correale, and Matthew I. Radnofsky, *Space Suit Development Status*, National Aeronautics and Space Administration, TND-3291, Washington, D.C., February, 1966; or Institute for Environmental Research and USAF Office of Scientific Research, *Symposium on Individual Cooling Process*, Kansas State University, Manhattan, Kansas, 1969.

Chapter 5   [1] "The Neanderthal Man Liked Flowers," *New York Times*, June 13, 1969, pp. 1, 47.

[2] George Santayana, *The Sense of Beauty* (New York: Dover Publications, Inc., 1955), p. 49. First published in 1896.

[3] Don Martindale, *American Society* (New York: D. Van Nostrand Company, Inc., 1960), p. 504.

[4] George P. Murdoch, "Universals of Culture," in *Readings in Anthropology*, ed. by E. Adamson Hoebel, Jesse D. Jennings, and Elmer R. Smith (New York: McGraw-Hill Book Company, 1955), pp. 4–5. Murdoch identifies the true universals of culture, not as identities in specific behavioral habits, but as similarities in classification of behavioral elements. One man may wear a dogskin cloak, another body paint, still another may scar his skin. All of their arts may be classified as body adornment.

[5] Charles Darwin, *The Voyage of the Beagle* (New York: Bantam Books, 1958), p. 177.

[6] Stanley D. Porteus, *The Psychology of a Primitive People* (New York: Longmans, Green and Co., 1931).

[7] Alexander Goldenweiser, "Limited Possibilities in Culture," in *Readings in Anthropology*, ed. by E. Adamson Hoebel, Jesse D. Jennings, and Elmer R. Smith (New York: McGraw-Hill Book Company, 1955), pp. 340–43.

[8] "A New Victory in the Battle Against Baldness," *Parade* (October 19, 1969), p. 27.

Chapter 6   [1] Bernard Rudofsky, "The Fashionable Body," *Horizon*, XIII, No. 4 (Autumn, 1971), 56.

[2] Kenneth Clark, *The Nude* (New York: Pantheon Books, 1956), pp. 20–21.

[3] Plato, *The Republic*, trans. Benjamin Jowett (New York: Books, Inc., 1943).

[4] LLOYD SHEARER, "Mini-Midi-Maxi—How Ridiculous Can Fashion Get," *Parade* (March 29, 1970), 5.

[5] MILLIA DAVENPORT, *The Book of Costume* (New York: Crown Publishers, 1948), II, 721.

[6] MARY ELIZA HAWEIS, *The Art of Dress* (London: Chatto and Windus, 1879), p. 32.

[7] MARILYN J. HORN, *The Second Skin* (Boston: Houghton Mifflin Co., 1968), p. 240; ALPHA LATZKE and HELEN P. HOSTETTER, *Wide World of Clothing* (New York: Ronald Press Company, 1968), p. 69.

[8] KOFI ANTUBAM, *Ghana's Heritage of Culture* (Leipzig: Koehler and Amelang, 1963), pp. 89–91.

[9] *Ibid.*, p. 92.

[10] *Ibid.*

[11] GRACE M. MORTON, *The Arts of Costume and Personal Appearance*, 3rd ed. rev. (New York: John Wiley and Sons, Inc., 1964), p. 31.

[12] JULIA MOCKETT PATRICK, *Distinctive Dress* (New York: Charles Scribner's Sons, 1969), p. 96.

[13] R. L. GREGORY, *Eye and Brain* (New York: McGraw-Hill Book Company, 1966), pp. 160–63.

Chapter 7

[1] Variations from these terms occur. For example, form is often used instead of shape, and lightness and darkness are sometimes used instead of value. However, the meanings of all the terms are generally well agreed upon.

[2] KENNETH CLARK, *The Nude* (New York: Pantheon Books, 1956), pp. 23–24.

[3] MARILYN REVELL DELONG, "Analysis of Costume Visual Form," *Journal of Home Economics*, LX (December, 1968), 784–88.

[4] MARILYN J. HORN, *The Second Skin* (Boston: Houghton Mifflin Company, 1968), pp. 237–38.

[5] MABEL D. ERWIN and LILA A. KINCHEN, *Clothing for Moderns*, 3rd ed. (New York: The Macmillan Company, 1964), p. 106.

[6] HELEN G. CHAMBERS and VERNA MOULTON, *Clothing Selection: Fashions, Figures, Fabrics* (New York: J. B. Lippincott Company, 1969), p. 74.

[7] HARRIET T. McJIMSEY, *Art in Clothing Selection* (New York: Harper and Row, 1963), pp. 72–73.

[8] P. THOMAS, *Kāma Kalpa or the Hindu Ritual of Love* (Bombay: D. B. Taraporevala Sons and Co., Private Ltd., n.d.), pp. 75–79.

Chapter 8

[1] RUTH BENEDICT, *Patterns of Culture* (Boston: Houghton Mifflin Co., 1959), p. 24.

[2] ORRIN E. KLAPP, *Heroes, Villains, and Fools* (Englewood Cliffs, N.J.: Prentice-Hall, Inc., 1962), p. 3.

[3] FREDERICK B. TOLLES, *Quakers and the Atlantic Culture* (New York: The Macmillan Company, 1960), p. 77.

[4] *Ibid*, pp. 77–78.

[5] MALCOLM MACDONALD, *People and Places* (London: Collins, 1969), p. 88.

[6] ALVIN TOFFLER, *Future Shock* (New York: Bantam Books, 1971), p. 307.

[7] *The Observer* (London), September 19, 1965.

[8] CAROLYN HUMPHREY, MARY KLAASEN, and ANNA M. CREEKMORE, "Clothing and Self-Concept of Adolescents," *Journal of Home Economics*, LXII, No. 4 (April, 1971), 246–50; and SUE HUNDLEY KUEHNE and ANNA M. CREEKMORE, "Relationships among Social Class, School Position, and Clothing of Adolescents," *Journal of Home Economics*, LXIII, No. 7 (October, 1971), 555–56.

[9] MEYER SCHAPIRO, "Taste," *The Encyclopaedia of the Social Sciences*, XIV (1934), 523.

[10] *Ibid.*

[11] MARILYN BENDER, *The Beautiful People* (New York: Dell Publishing Co., Inc., 1967), pp. 79–81.

Chapter 9

[1] GIULIA VERONESI, *Into the Twenties: Style and Design 1909–1929* (London: Thames and Hudson, 1968).

[2] AGNES BROOKS YOUNG, *Stage Costuming* (New York: The Macmillan Company, 1927), p. 1–2.

[3] JOAN LAWSON and PETER REVITT, *Dressing for the Ballet* (London: Adam and Charles Black, 1958), pp. 5–6.

[4] LAWRENCE LANGNER, *The Importance of Wearing Clothes* (New York: Hastings House, 1959), p. 266.

[5] HELENA CHALMERS, *Clothes On and Off the Stage* (New York: D. Appleton & Co., 1928), p. 5.

[6] PATRICIA MCCORMACK, "Circus Attire Design Keyed to Maintenance," *State Journal* (Lansing-East Lansing, Michigan), March 26, 1971, p. B–3.

[7] LANGNER, *op. cit.*, p. 242.

[8] LEON BRAUNER, "Character Portrayal through Costume," *Proceedings of the Eleventh Conference of College Teachers of Clothing, Textiles and Related Arts,* Western Region, Utah State University, October 15–17, 1964, pp. 23–26.

[9] WINIFRED H. MILLS and LOUISE M. DUNN, *Marionettes, Masks and Shadows* (New York: Doubleday, Doran & Co., 1928), p. 168.

[10] LANGNER, *op. cit.*, p. 242

[11] "The Old Age of Dustin Hoffman," *Life,* LXIX (November 20, 1970), p. 78.

[12] GUSTAVE FLAUBERT, *Madame Bovary,* trans. Eleanor Mary Aveling (New York: The Modern Library, 1950), pp. 57–58.

[13] ROBERT HERRICK, "Upon Julia's Clothes."

[14] MARY BARELLI GALLAGHER, *My Life with Jacqueline Kennedy* (New York: Paperback Library Edition, 1969), p. 93.

[15] MAYA ANGELOU, *I Know Why the Caged Bird Sings* (New York: Bantam Book Edition, 1969), pp. 1–2.

Chapter 10   [1] Others have used the term post-industrial, or advanced industrial instead of mass society; tribal, nonliterate, and primitive have been used instead of folk.

[2] ROBERT REDFIELD, "The Folk Society," *The American Journal of Sociology,* LII, No. 4 (January, 1947), 293–308.

[3] REGINA G. TWALA, "Beads as Regulating the Social Life of the Zulu and Swazi," *African Studies,* X (1951), 120.

[4] PAUL BOHANNAN, "Beyond Civilization," Supplement of *Natural History,* February, 1971, p. 5.

Chapter 11   [1] PHILIP OLSON, *The Study of Modern Society* (New York: Random House, 1970), p. 143.

[2] *How American Buying Habits Change* (Washington, D.C.: U.S. Department of Labor, 1959), p. 134.

[3] R. GALLETTI, K. D. S. BALDWIN, and I. O. DINA, "Clothing of Nigerian Cocoa Farmers' Families," in *Dress, Adornment and the Social Order,* ed. by Mary Ellen Roach and Joanne Bubolz Eicher (New York: John Wiley and Sons, 1965), pp. 91–92. Also in GALLETTI, et al., *Nigerian Cocoa Farmers* (Oxford: Oxford University Press, 1956), pp. 246–52.

[4] "A Superior Sort of Liar," *Time,* LXXII, No. 26 (June 29, 1959), 84;

ROBERT CRICHTON, "Uproarious Trip with the Master Imposter," *Life*, XLVII (July 6, 1959), 96.

[5] DON MARTINDALE, *American Society* (Princeton, N. J.: D. Van Nostrand Company, Inc., 1960), p. 19.

[6] *Journal of the Apparel Research Foundation*, II, No. 3 (1967) 12, 23; IV, No. 2 (1970) 3, 7; and II, No. 1 (1967) 4, 5, 20, 22.

[7] *Ibid*, III, No. 3 (1969), 32.

[8] *Ibid*, III, No. 2 (1969), 2.

[9] *Ibid*, V, No. 1 (1971), 1–11.

[10] DANIEL J. BOORSTEIN, "Welcome to the Consumption Community," *Fortune*, September 1, 1967, pp. 118–20, 131–38.

[11] ORRIN E. KLAPP, *Collective Search for Identity* (New York: Holt, Rinehart, and Winston Inc., 1969), pp. 73–115.

[12] RALPH LINTON, "Primitive Art," in *Every Man His Way*, ed. by Alan Dundes (Englewood Cliffs, N. J.: Prentice-Hall, Inc., 1968), p. 356.

[13] PAUL S. WINGERT, *Primitive Art* (New York: The World Publishing Company, 1965, A Meridian Book), p. 61.

Chapter 12   [1] The *1971 World Population Data Sheet* reports population growth for all but one of the 5 countries listed, and cites a current world population growth rate of 2.0. At this rate of growth, world population will double in 35 years. *World Population Data Sheet* (Washington, D.C.: Population Reference Bureau, Inc., Revised edition, Ausust, 1971). Bogue explains that population growth is the result of births exceeding deaths and/or in-migration exceeding out-migration. The growth rate is calculated by dividing the population increase during the year by the population at the beginning of the year and converting the decimal to a percent. See: Donald J. Bogue, *Principles of Demgraphy* (New York: John Wiley and Sons, Inc., 1969), pp. 35, 37.

[2] ROBERT L. HEILBRONER, *The Making of Economic Society* (Englewood Cliffs, N.J.: Prentice-Hall, Inc., 1962), pp. 4–5.

[3] LLOYD G. REYNOLDS, *Economics, a General Introduction* (Homewood, Ill.: Richard D. Irwin, Inc., 1963), p. 14.

[4] Fiber quantity, source and use, see: "Raw Fiber Equivalent of Imports and Exports of Man-made Fiber, Cotton and Wool Manufactures," *Textile Organon*, XXXVII, No. 3 (1966), 53; and XL, No. 3 (1969), 53; and "Textile Fiber End Use Survey," *Textile Organon*, XLI, No. 1 (1970), 3–5. The U.A.R., Mexico, Peru and India were the largest cotton exporters to the United States in the early 1960s, see: "Imports for Consumption and General Imports of Merchandise, Commodity by Country of Origin: 1961 to 1963,"

Foreign Commerce and Navigation of the United States 1946–1963 (Washington, D.C.: U. S. Government Printing Office, U.S. Department of Commerce, Bureau of the Census, 1965), p. 332. Average yields per acre from 1963–67, see: "Cotton: Acreage, Yield, and Production in Specified Countries, Average 1963–67, Annual 1968 and 1969," *Cotton Situation* (Washington, D.C.: U.S. Government Printing Office, U.S. Department of Agriculture, Economic Research Service, March 1970), p. 38.

[5] SANFORD D. GORDON, GEORGE G. DAWSON, and JESS WITCHEL, *The American Economy, Analysis and Policy* (Lexington, Mass.: D.C. Heath and Company, 1969), p. 6.

[6] EDWARD B. ESPENSHADE, JR., ed., *Goode's World Atlas,* 12th ed., revised (Chicago: Rand McNally & Co., 1964), p. 32; *Encyclopedia Britannica* (1969), VI, 613 and IX, 430; R. E. H. MELLOR, *Geography of the U.S.S.R.* (New York: St. Martin's Press, 1966), pp. 196, 207; J. RUSSELL SMITH and M. OGDEN PHILLIPS, *Industrial and Commercial Geography,* 3rd ed. (New York: Henry Holt and Co., 1946) pp. 619–23.

[7] WILBUR ZELINSKY, *A Prologue to Population Geography* (Englewood Cliffs, N. J.: Prentice-Hall, Inc., 1966), p. 102.

[8] *World Population Data Sheet, op. cit.;* DONALD BREMMER, "Indonesia Plagued by High Birthrate," *State Journal* (Lansing-East Lansing, Michigan), July 11, 1971, p. F–4.

[9] *Encyclopedia Britannica* (1969), XXIII, 663.

[10] Developing nation is a term used to describe countries which are relatively less prosperous and non-industrialized; examples are the countries of Latin America, Africa and Asia. Synonyms are "low income," "have nots," and "less developed countries."

[11] HEILBRONER, *op. cit.,* pp. 9–14.

[12] REYNOLDS, *op. cit.,* p. 44.

[13] KENNETH MACLEISH, "Help for Philippine Tribes in Trouble," *National Geographic Magazine,* CXL, No. 2 (August, 1971), 232–39.

[14] *Encyclopedia Britannica* (1964), XII, 188, 190; SYDNEY H. SCHANBERG, "Untouchables in Rural India Seek Better Life," *State Journal* (Lansing-East Lansing, Michigan), November 15, 1970, p. F–4.

[15] REYNOLDS, *op. cit.,* pp. 53–54.

[16] B. GAFUROV, "Toward New Advance in Soviet Cotton Growing," *Pravda,* January 16, 1953, p. 2; These Things Will Be Made of Cotton," *Sovetskoye Khlopkovodstvo* (Ministry of Cotton Growing), December 24, 1952, p. 2. Condensed and translated by the *Current Digest of the Soviet Press* (Ann Arbor, Michigan: The Joint Committee on Slavic Studies), V, Part 1, No. 4, 14–41.

[17] YE. CHERNYKH and MIKH. DOLGOPOLOV, "Spring and Fashions," *Izvestia,* May 6, 1961, p. 4. Cond. and trans. *Current Digest of the Soviet Press, op. cit.,* XIII, Part 2, No. 18, 24, 25.

[18] Much information about the Soviet system is available in the *Current Digest of the Soviet Press,* a weekly English translation of selected contents of *Pravda, Izvestia* and approximately 60 other Soviet newspapers and magazines. The translations, many of the entire text, are presented without editorial comment with the intent of providing objective information. See: *Current Digest of the Soviet Press, op. cit.,* XXIII, No. 43 (November 23, 1971), 40.

[19] CHERNYKH and DOLGOPOLOV, *op. cit.,* p. 24.

[20] L. YEFREMOVA and A. LEVASHOVA, "Economics of Beauty," *Izvestia,* April 5, 1964. Complete text trans. *Current Digest of the Soviet Press, op. cit.,* XVI, Part 2, No. 14, 31–32.

[21] N. NAGAITSEVA, "Why Do Inferior Goods Get into the Stores?" *Trud,* January 15, 1953, p. 2. Cond. and trans. *Current Digest of the Soviet Press, op. cit.,* V, Part 1, No. 3, 34; CHERNYKH and DOLGOPOLOV, *op. cit.,* p. 24.

[22] HEILBRONER, *op. cit.,* pp. 58–68.

[23] *Labor in the Textile and Apparel Industries* (Washington, D.C.: U.S. Government Printing Office, U.S. Department of Labor, Bureau of Labor Statistics), Bulletin No. 1635, August, 1969, pp. 5–7.

[24] JESSICA DAVES, *Ready-made Miracle* (New York: G. P. Putnam's Sons, 1967), pp. 54–101.

[25] "The Union Opinion," *Femme-Lines* (May–June, 1971), pp. 24, 27.

[26] U. S. estimates of fiber consumption may prove low because in 1969 a level of 51 pounds per capita was reached. See Virginia Britton, "Clothing and Textiles: Supplies, Prices and Outlook for 1971," paper presented at the Consumer and Food Economics Research Division, National Agricultural Outlook Conference, Washington, D.C., U.S. Department of Agriculture, Agricultural Research Service.

[27] "Agricultural Commodity Projections for 1975 and 1985," *Monthly Bulletin of Agricultural Economics and Statistics* (FAO), XVI, No. 11 (November, 1967), 9.

[28] "Cotton, Wool, and Man-made Fibers: Aggregate Consumption in High-Income Countries, Estimated by Principal End-Uses," *Agricultural Commodity Projections, 1970–1980* (FAO), Rome, 1971, II, Statistical Appendix, 51–2.

Chapter 13   [1] BERNARD GWERTZMAN, "In Russia It's the 'In' Thing to Debate Fads," *New York Times,* August 6, 1971, p. 2.

[2] JOSEPHINE WOOD and LILLY DE JONGH OSBORNE, *Indian Costume of Guatemala*, (Graz: Akademische Druck-u Verlagsanstalt, 1966), p. ix.

[3] KEIICHIRO NAKAGAWA and HENRY ROSOVSKY, "The Case of the Dying Kimono: The Influence of Changing Fashions of the Japanese Woolen Industry," *Business History Review*, XXXVII (Spring-Summer, 1963), 66.

[4] GERALDINE MEERBOTT made this observation in a class presentation at Michigan State University.

[5] *Life*, LXXI, No. 20 (November 12, 1971), 30.

[6] "Masai Told to Wear Trousers," *State Journal* (Lansing-East Lansing, Michigan), September 12, 1971, p. E-13.

[7] GWERTZMAN, *op. cit.*, p. 2.

[8] RUDI GERNREICH, "Fashion for the '70s," *Life*, LXVII, No. 1 (January 9, 1970), pp. 115–18.

[9] "What Fashion Designer John Weitz Sees Ahead," *Textile World*, CXVIII, No. 4 (April, 1968), 199.

INDEX

241